The Antichrist: The Grand Plan of Total Global Enslavement

Dan Desmarques

Published by 22 Lions Publishing, 2020.

Table of Contents

Copyright Page. 1

Introduction. 3

Chapter 01: A Special Acknowledgement. 5

Chapter 02: Why Was This Book Written? 7

Chapter 03: Can This Book Be a Prophetic Warning? 9

Chapter 04: The Purpose of the False Prophets. 11

Chapter 05: There is No More Time! 13

Chapter 06. How to Understand Demonic Possession? 15

Chapter 07: Are Humans Originally Good or Bad? 17

Chapter 08: The Problem with Narcissism. 21

Chapter 09: Reality is a Self-Projection! 23

Chapter 10: How are We Controlled by Our Impulses? 25

Chapter 11: Why is Communism Evil? 29

Chapter 12: Why is Money Not Evil? 31

Chapter 13: Why are People Mentally Enslaved? 33

Chapter 14: The War on Awareness. 35

Chapter 15: How Beliefs Keep People Poor and Stupid. 37

Chapter 16: Capitalism is a Luxury of the Smartest! 39

Chapter 17: Stupidity is a Contagious Disease! 41

Chapter 18: Being Dumb is a Choice! 45

Chapter 19: The War on Information! 47

Chapter 20: Can We Be Kind to Others? 49

Chapter 21: Why are Most People So Ignorant? 53

Chapter 22: Can Humans Be Enslaved? 57

Chapter 23: Why Do People Agree with a Dumb Logic? 59

Chapter 24: The Neo-Anarchists. 61

Chapter 25: The Use of Psychology Against The People. 65

Chapter 26: The Eradication of the Individuality. 67

Chapter 27: The Corruption of the Religious Faith. 69

Chapter 28: The Plan for Total Global Enslavement. 71

Chapter 29: Voices in Our Head? 73

Chapter 30: The Book of Revelation and Israel? 77

Chapter 31: The Illegal State of the Zionists. 81

Chapter 32: The War for the Control of Public Health. 85

Chapter 33: Philanthropic Colonialism and Eugenics. 89

Chapter 34: The Technocratic Dictatorship. 91

Chapter 35: Satan's Witchcraft. 93

Chapter 36: The Gates Foundation. 97

Chapter 37: Philanthropic Colonialism and Censorship. 101

Chapter 38: The Myth of Overpopulation 105

Chapter 39: The Biological Warfare Against the Masses. 109

Chapter 40: The AI View on Spirituality. 111

Chapter 41: Can the AI Create a Global Religion? 115

Chapter 42: The AI-God. 119

Chapter 43: Who Are the Raelians? 123

Chapter 44: The Misinformation Agents. 127

Chapter 45: How to Identify the False Prophets? 131

Chapter 46: Religious Atheism and Spiritual Prostitution. 135

Chapter 47: The Suppression of Mass Consciousness. 139

Chapter 48: The Challenge in Being Oneself. 141

Chapter 49: The Great Scam of the Psychiatric Industry. 145

Chapter 50: A Circus of Clowns Named Scientology. 147

Chapter 51: Why Do Scientologists Act Like Criminals? 151

Chapter 52. Why Scientology Only Wants Your Money? 153

Chapter 53. Religions are Corporations! 155

Chapter 54. When Satan Pays for Your Bible! 157

Chapter 55: The Infiltration of Religious Organizations. 161

Chapter 56: The Best Kept Secret in Scientology. 165

Chapter 57: Why the CIA Wants Scientology? 167

Chapter 58: Who Murdered the Founder of Scientology? 171

Chapter 59: What Scientologists Don't Want You to Know. 173

Chapter 60: The Question Scientologists Never Answer! 177

Chapter 61: The Illusion of Salvation. 181

Chapter 62: Thinking Positive and Being Unconscious. 183

Chapter 63: Why Love Became a Rare Commodity? 187

Chapter 64: Why People Don't Want to Show Compassion?.........................189

Chapter 65: Are Modern Christians Capable of Loving Others?..................191

Chapter 66: The Chosen Ones. 195

Chapter 67: The Choice that is Asked!..197

Chapter 68: The Leaders of The New World Order....................................201

Chapter 69: The Secret Mind Control Experiments...................................205

Chapter 70: MK-Ultra and The Jonestown Massacre.................................209

Chapter 71: Mind Control Technology and Radio-Frequency.....................213

Chapter 72: Beyond The Mind Control Technology. 217

Chapter 73: The Use of Games by Intelligence Agencies............................221

Chapter 74: How Facebook Became A Global Threat. 225

Chapter 75: How the AI Monitors Thoughts and Emotions. 229

Chapter 76: The Mark 666 and Nanotechnology. 231

Chapter 77: The Last Days on Earth. 233

Chapter 78: The Secret Space Program...237

Chapter 79: The Angels of Christ. 239

Chapter 80: The Judgement Day. 243

Chapter 81: God and the Gods. 247

Bibliography..251

Copyright Page.

The Antichrist: The Grand Plan of Total Global Enslavement

By Dan Desmarques

Copyright © Dan Desmarques, 2020 (1st Ed.) All Rights Reserved.

Introduction.

Many exorcists have pointed out that the amount of people possessed by demons has significantly increased in the past years. But it is important to noice, as exorcist Fr. Francesco Bamonte said, that "Satan is not the god of evil against the God of the good, rather he is a being who God created as good. Satan and the spirits at his service, therefore, are not omnipotent beings, they cannot perform miracles, they are not omnipresent, they cannot know our thoughts or know the future".

The acknowledgement of our thoughts and the control over the human mind, has to be given, and necessarily come from the outside. And that can only be facilitated with the aid of science, namely, psychiatry, technology, and the progress made by the social sciences as a whole in the understanding of the human behavior and its predictability, along with the identification of the human desires and impulses.

It is in this latest point, that we find religion to be an excellent means of study and experimentation. For it is here that we notice an interconnection of different elements of the human nature in an open display attributed to faith and trust. In other words, the Antichrist will have to manifest himself through a religion. But not without the aid of mind control techniques. And this is why Satan needs to operate through many areas in order to make his plan of total global cnslavement possible.

In this book, you will see exactly how this plan is being developed for the past decades, and how different religions are working towards making it a reality. The book guarantees to forever destroy your childlike and naive version of reality. For it will present you with abundant evidence of an acceleration in the process of creating a universal religion with the intention of enslaving mankind. Here you will be offered facts, and not just theories, related to the plan that has been unfolding, so that you may be able to see it for yourself.

This is not a book based on faith or religion, but rather scientific and historical events interconnected for a specific purpose — global enslavement.

Chapter 01: A Special Acknowledgement.

Before we move towards what I have learned over the past twenty years of my life, analyzing this topic with multiple religions, and in many countries, I want to give special thanks. Special thanks to all the morons who obsess over their bible but refuse to help with anything that consists in providing useful information to the world, because they are too preoccupied with going to heaven and don't believe anything outside what the bible shows them, or are told to believe in regards to the same book. They made me realize how useless a religion can be and how pathetic fanatics have become. As studies show, religion can indeed be formed out of a bunch of hypocrites. And as I have understood, you don't have to be a christian to be inside a christian congregation. You can even preach that which you don't practice.

Among all the christian groups I have encountered, the most cynical and hypocritical of them all, is certainly the Jehovah Witnesses. If their God likes them, Satan has nothing to do.

I wish to give special thanks as well, to the social awkward who spend entire days posting information on social media with the claim that they're trying to save the world, but refuse to help in a research, just because my help can have more impact than theirs and they don't want to be left behind. They made me realize how desperate the ostracized are for a little validation.

Special thanks to those who who organize social events but insult me when I try to do something useful for the same people. They made me realize that their egotistic needs are far more important to them, and that they don't really care about anyone else but themselves.

Special thanks to those who insist that I sell drugs, rather than spend entire days in front of my computer trying to finish books that they will never read. They made me realize how mentally small many people are, even when having college degrees. If the world depended on such graduates, the human race would already be extinct.

DAN DESMARQUES

Special thanks to the many women whom I loved and abandoned me for thinking I'm psychopathic, weird or antisocial. They showed me that being myself and not tolerating ignorance can make me rich, while pleasing them would make me miserable in three ways — financial, emotional and mental. Being a brainwashed moron has its consequences, but I rather lose pseudo-relationships based on female greed than turning into a well-adjusted moron.

Special thanks to the many coffee shop baristas from Poland who treated me badly for spending more time in their workplace than most of their clients. They made me realize that the newest generations can be useless even for a common job as simple as serving coffee, and that the brainwashed will never understand any explanation of mine.

Special thanks to the computer technicians of Lithuania who refused to fix my computer several times, and for xenophobic reasons, or the Lithuanian security guards, that threatened me for confusing me with a Russian spy, just because I decided to spend three hours of a morning reading a book in a public place. The Lithuanians, among which these are just some of the many examples I could offer, made me realize that some countries do deserve to be turned into ashes for whatsoever reason and for the common wellbeing of humanity.

Or maybe we can just let this nation — already world number one in death rates by suicide — finish itself in its own imbecility. Or should I say boredom? Because human sacrifices were a common practice here, and until only a few centuries ago, showing us that psychopathy can indeed be a cultural and widespread trait, as I've never seen so many sick people in one single location. I thank them for showing me that reality can surpass the wildest fiction.

I truly want to say thanks to all these people, who participated in my reality for the past years, and that, even though representing a small sample of the world, when compared to the many billions, show us why there is this vast contamination of ignorance on Earth, and justifying the spiritual, intellectual and emotional misery in which many live today.

Stupidity is truly the most widespread disease! No virus will ever match that!

Chapter 02: Why Was This Book Written?

Many times I wondered what was the purpose of writing these books, taking into consideration that most of this planet is filled with ignorance, lack of consideration, disrespect and apathetic individuals. And this, just as much as I often questioned myself as to why the Freemasons and Rosicrucians — many of whom, among those I met, with over 80 years old — still hold on to their secrets and refuse to answer my most simple questions. For it is as if they didn't expect their beliefs on reincarnation to manifest, resulting in their own coming back and facing the results of what they are doing.

It is impressive to see so many members of Secret Societies considering themselves important, and above their own doctrine, immersed in a delusional arrogance. And this, while they commonly act like a pathetic group without any awareness of the world in which they live.

After stupidity, arrogance must be the second most widespread disease.

The disease of arrogance, has reached the depths of the most self-protected religious congregations and cults too, no matter how many security guards they keep at the entrance of their temples.

Could this be the reason why so many Scientologists and members of the Jehovah Witnesses claim to want to save the world, when in fact they spend far more time investigating my own personal life and fearing my knowledge, while giving me no relevant answers?

Somehow, their concept of help seems to always get filtered by their egotistic views on reality. And yet, I thank them, for showing me that we don't share the same God or even the same conceptualization of the meaning of "help".

We live in a world that seems dead already. Most people are merely occupying space at this point. They will never change. They don't care about changing. They are too selfish to go beyond their own delusional mind and views of the world.

Religion can't do anything for them either. And their concept of salvation should be included in the DSM — Diagnostic and Statistical Manual of Mental Disorders — because the written accusations I have made to the leadership of many of these groups, including the ones named here, for violating their own ethical codes, and that resulted in a complete silence, say everything about their real moral level — None, Nada, Zero.

Funny how these people preach values that they themselves consider to be above the obligation of following!

If narcissism was chocolate, they would all be morbidly obese! But I thank them, for forcing me to focus on my own work and mission on Earth, even if that was never their intention.

What I am doing with my books is, as I have concluded, the only alternative to a very sick planet.

I wish there were more authors presenting the truth at the level that I am presenting it, but if that was the case, the proportion of ignorant minds wouldn't be so vast, and I wouldn't be called a prophet so many times either.

Yes, I am a prophet, in the context in which we live. But I wish I wasn't! I wish I could just be a musician in a planet where compassion, empathy and respect for human life and spiritual development was the norm.

It is hard to believe that God wants me to write these books for the majority, and as much as I can't call them human. They are the walking dead! But I thank them for showing me that my anger is the result of frustration. For I cannot wake the dead!

Very few people on this planet are worth my time and energy, and it is only for these that I write these books; It is because of them that I battle for the truth! For the rest is truly lost!

I wrote this book for you, because I believe you did not find this book by coincidence. And I thank you, my reader, for proceeding, and reading it:

Thank You!

Chapter 03: Can This Book Be a Prophetic Warning?

I wrote this book simply because that is what I came to this planet to do.

I am here to leave the only bible worth reading — my own collection of scriptures!

I am certainly being sarcastic and truthful at the same time, when saying this, despite the many who would think I am an arrogant or narcissistic.

I rather be an honest narcissist and truthful element of history than a dumb parasite. For I have no more reasons to apply false modesty, or time to keep wasting, pretending I am not who I am.

On the other hand, the best judgment of our actions comes from those we attract. And I am proud to see that many of my readers appear to be an amazing group of awaken souls with the kindest hearts.

They are indeed my religion. But I did not choose them. God did! My God! For I do not know to what kind of God everyone else is praying.

I consider this God I follow to be the ruler of the whole Universe. He is not inside one book or one little house called temple. He doest not belong to a group of schizophrenics and is not determined by hierarchies or beliefs.

This God, does not discriminate the prostitutes or the homosexual, or the ugly and fat, or even the ignorant and retarded. He doesn't even discriminate the criminals or the poor and spiritually blind.

He is the Light that covers all of the Earth and reaches the deepest darkness within our soul, as well as the darkest heart. He is the true God of All Miracles!

Only this God can bring light to the most agonizing pains, and insights to the most deserving spirits.

These words come from such holy and inspirational insights.

DAN DESMARQUES

I would not be able to identify the liars, the fake prophets and the signs of the Antichrist with my intellect only, and without the help of such Mighty God. For many religions have been deceived already.

This said, may you feel such Light in my words, either you call him a He or a She. For this God is not an Hermaphrodite, Heterosexual or Homosexual, or Bisexual, or even Sapiosexual. He doesn't belong to the distorting thoughts of the human kind. Even though He desperately needs a new church brought forth from all the corners of the Earth; a church formed with the survivors of this apocalypse of stupidity and narcissism, and which has already started.

You see, most people are already dead; they just don't know it; they are unaware of their decadence, and merely walk around like living corpses. But the One Truth, however, will never perish.

If you find my books, you also find this Truth!

Chapter 04: The Purpose of the False Prophets.

The fact that I despise nearly all of the self-proclaimed prophets on Earth and will promptly call them liars, doesn't mean that I wish to have a combat for souls with them. For they are fulfilling the goal of drifting the lost cattle to the slaughterhouse.

Many of the most famous authors out there, such as Eckhart Tolle, are possessed by demons. And yet, people follow them. As much as they follow many others, that are nothing more than disturbing narcissists craving for attention, like mad wolves in a forest filled with dumb sheep.

The Bible — Matthew 7:15 — warns about such people. Yes, most still can't identify them. The Bible says: "Beware of false prophets, which come to you in sheep's clothing, but inwardly are ravening wolves."

What can 'sheep's clothing refer to'?

It refers to those who appear to be harmless, use soft words, and seem to have compassion for others, while deceiving and manipulating the ignorant masses.

Personally, I don't even claim for sheep. For I am a shepherd of awakened souls, that are independent enough to think for themselves and make their own decisions.

My purpose is to make such decisions effective and aligned with Universal Truth.

I will never determine such decisions or make them my own. People are free to think for themselves. And if they can't do that, if they can't acknowledge the Truth, then it is not my business to redirect them towards me. For I do not educate anymore at this point.

I don't think there is much time left for that!

My purpose is to merely awaken those who are ready to be awakened!

Those who can be enlightened shall be enlightened!

The ones who are already dead, can't be awaken any longer. They are just waiting for the final end.

On the another hand, I wouldn't be sent to Earth, if such people weren't so abundant on the planet, because, in truth, I do not belong here.

I do not, however, claim the title of prophet or guru, because it is irrelevant to those who do not read my work or do not trust it.

I am only a prophet and guru to those who follow me and trust me. And to them, the God I worship belongs. Because I am just a messenger. Nothing more than that!

The rest will always show a predisposition to follow a false God — the architect of delusional minds.

That God doesn't exist except in the collective imaginary. Such people could pray to a Virtual God inside a video game and notice no difference.

That is why the Bible warns (In Matthew 24:24) about a deception — in the last days —, so great, that it will deceive even the chosen ones.

Chapter 05: There is No More Time!

Over the years, I have released more truths about myself, and what I think of this world, than I did before. And I did so, because I believe there is no more time left — before a final judgement.

We have come to the end of this game called life.

I still write but, now, to create followers. For this planet doesn't exist anymore as it once was, and freedom is truly gone.

The idea of freedom, as these pages will show you, is now a product of the imaginary.

For this reason, I do not discriminate those who take justice in their hands, and are willing to die for a cause. I do not discriminate those who understand the value of moral over pettiness. I do not discriminate radicalism in the name of the One Truth.

This Truth doesn't belong to any egotistically-centered mind. It belongs to the future! For when everyone, currently alive, is one day dead, this Truth will persist. And, if it is welcomed, the dead shall resurrect — as awakened spirits that can remember their past lives — and truly know they are immortal. For as much as the truth is immortal, so is the soul, and so are my words.

I wish nothing but peace and happiness to those who trust these words. For the anger that an awakening may cause, is only the result of a long suppressed frustration towards creating a better world.

Many have lost their life for the freedoms we enjoy today! Such choice shouldn't be part of our life anymore. But, sadly, it still is! We still need to fight to maintain our freedom. Although, the greatest attack right now, is on the overall awareness. It is a psychological attack!

Hopefully, may words will enlighten you and protect you from such attack. For "World War III is a guerrilla information war with no division between military and civilian participation" (Marshall McLuhan, In Culture Is Our Business).

Chapter 06. How to Understand Demonic Possession?

The world has been preparing the coming of the Antichrist for at least two thousand years, and many believe that he or she is not here yet, on Earth, because the signs of the holy books have not been fully presented.

However, as many exorcists have mentioned, the amount of people possessed by demons keeps increasing. And as this book will show you, such isn't a coincidence, for these demonically possessed individuals are preparing the route for the others — at a mental, emotional and even physical level.

The current Chairman of the International Association of Exorcists, Father Francesco Bamonte, frequently stresses that present times are exceptional, as far as the activity of the forces of evil goes. According to Bamonte, "A typical behavior of the devil during the exorcism is to often talk about destruction and annihilation. All that is beautiful, good, healthy, pure, harmonious is mocked and threatened with extinction and destruction". And so, one can assume that the devil opposes love, empathy and any demonstration of affection.

A truly diabolical religion, would have to somehow deny such values and, in order to be accepted by the masses, match these same values in society.

As we see, more and more people feel lonely and depressed, because more people show signs of selfishness, depression, narcissism and lack of empathy for others.

It is this denial of empathy and absence of love for others that leads one to immerse himself in the possibility of getting possessed.

According to Father Vincent Lampert — exorcist in Indianapolis, United States —, "There are many people who laugh at the notion of demonic possession or even the reality itself, but the Catholic Church does teach that evil is a reality and it is personified in the person of the Devil" (In an interview to Vice).

Possession has been clearly divided between belief and disbelief, which grants more time for the Devil to possess a soul. For what one can't see, he can't defend himself from.

It is important to noice, as Fr. Francesco Bamonte has said, that "Satan and the spirits at his service,... cannot know our thoughts or know the future". This acknowledgement of thoughts and the control of the human mind, have to come through science, technology and the progress made by the social sciences in studying human behavior.

The Antichrist has to manifest itself with the help of mind control techniques. And this is why Satan needs to operate through many areas to make his plan of total global enslavement possible.

Father Gary Thomas, from The Ministry of Exorcisms warned, in a public speech that, "The demonic can also travel through demonic currents. That does not mean that one's computer can be possessed, but it does mean that the images processed by technology can have a huge detrimental effect. Because of the effect on the brain... Like Violent video games. What becomes mainstream, becomes part of the culture, and when certain things become part of the culture, they look harmless."

As our cultures become more and more controlled and manipulated by the forces of evil, many things that become seen as normal, then create the conditions for a complete mental and spiritual possession.

Chapter 07: Are Humans Originally Good or Bad?

Do good people become evil? Or are evil people born evil? Can evil people become good? And are people truly good or evil, or that depends only in our perception of good and evil?

I have asked myself these questions many times. And I admit, I'm usually very naive in what regards finding the answer. Because most of my personal problems, appear due to the fact that I tend to trust blindly in others.

I do the opposite of other people. Most people start with distrust when meeting someone for the first time, and I start with trust. I always love and trust until I have a reason not to. And so, I've been betrayed and insulted badly and often. But this is my nature.

As an empath, it is hard to change this predisposition, with which many empaths can identify with. Empaths naturally want to associate with people. And can't understand why so many would immediately assume that the world is out to kill them.

This paranoia, and constant fear that most people live with, is psychopathic. Most people are indeed paranoid and psychopathic. But that is now the norm. As such, empaths are viewed as fools and weak souls. But are they?

People seem to always attack that which confuses them and they can't understand or assimilate as being normal. It's part of human nature to do that, or at least, our most basic and primitive instincts. And most people are there, at that level of basic instincts.

They have not overcome their reptilian brain. They have not evolved beyond it. Their life is composed of repetitions and cycles of what seems familiar. They fear what is unknown. And that is why xenophobia and racism is on the rise. Stupidity is on the rise with it, and everything else that comes out of it, is simply a consequence of being stupid.

Love, for the stupid, can be, very confusing, if it doesn't include some form of exchange and the fulfillment of expectations. Because their self-centered attention cannot understand the value of empathy.

Their mind is limited to the now and the "me". As such, the level of consciousness of such people has been tremendously limited.

What people watch in the movies and the type of education that they get from school, the majority of the friends they associate with, and the lessons they get at home, are all conditioning them towards a very limiting and selfish, even narcissistic, approach to life.

When someone then feels like a failure, and has reduced existence to getting something, anything goes, and the soul becomes a metaphysical topic that they don't wish even to talk about.

Talking about the soul, or even God, becomes a confrontation with consciousness that they can't handle. And so, they push such individuals away.

Truly many people have stopped talking to me when I mentioned the word "God" or when I said that "pride" and "fame" means nothing to me, because I am not trying to be appreciated by others. Some have even called me stupid, for saying that I don't wish to become popular.

Most people, right now, are so obsessed with themselves, that they will literally stop talking to you, if you mention anything beyond that — them.

One of these examples that I am referring to, is a woman dying from cancer. She is still obsessed with posting photos on social media, and having men telling her how beautiful she is. That is still her priority in life.

When I mentioned the word 'God' in one of our conversations, and then 'faith', she stopped talking to me.

Basically, people make themselves good and bad. And from what I have observed, this applies also to those who keep posting biblical quotes as if they were saints.

THE ANTICHRIST: THE GRAND PLAN OF TOTAL GLOBAL ENSLAVEMENT

Truly many religious people are as evil as one can imagine. Most, are psychopathic and narcissistic. Because now, they get that narcissistic rush from their own congregation too, telling them constantly that they are superior to the rest of society.

Chapter 08: The Problem with Narcissism.

The vast majority is so obsessed with themselves, that they don't care about their own health, their mind or their spirit. They are incredibly stupid and they will be stupid for as long as they live. They will never ever change. But can people change?

Yes, people can change. But would a person, that is narcissistic and obsessed with what others think, change?

No, that will never happen. Because changing at this point, means losing all that admiration and attention, even if it is fake, and even if it kills them.

This is why so many celebrities rather hang themselves or overdose on drugs and painkillers instead of losing their narcissistic supply of attention.

Attention is a powerful drug. Many people who have never had anything in their life, crave attention more than they crave love. Love cannot give them the same quick rush that a powerful injection of attention does.

Social media, with all its tricks and tools, has increased the value of this narcissistic attention. That is why so many women compete for it, by posting naked or semi-naked photos of themselves online.

Men, on the other hand, have made themselves obsessed with their body and appearance, more than their achievements.

Society is now more superficial than ever and at a great cost. Having a normal conversation with someone became nearly impossible.

Most people can't even talk without analyzing everything they say in their brain first, and after analyzing what someone else says. Conversations turned into a kind of artificial, almost cybernetic, collection and analysis of data, rather than a heart to heart interaction.

Most people I know, only text me when I am traveling, or in other words, when I post a photo related to something they admire and want. Their friendship is based on what I can do for them, my social and informational value — my social worth from their point of view, and not who I am as a person. Who I really am, means nothing to them.

Let us not be fooled, for there is a predisposition, on the vast majority, to be jealous and to resent anyone who is better than them in any way, either financially, mentally or emotionally.

People tend to hate those who are richer, smarter and happier. Even though this predisposition has been conditioned in them. They are brainwashed.

This condition is what leads us to the complexity of the questions we ask about human nature. For if nearly 8 billion souls are conditioned to hate each other, can we truly speak of a human nature that is so rare that becomes an exception?

You see, what is normal is often confused with what is common. And so, maybe now we can see that it is common for humans to be jealous, selfish and evil, but is it normal?

We all want to be loved, respected and appreciated. This seems normal, for survival purposes, and for our well-being in general. And so, we can say that most people on Earth are abnormal, mentally sick, even retarded from an evolutionary point of view.

Chapter 09: Reality is a Self-Projection!

I have realized, over the course of my life, that most of what is blamed on the Power Elite, comes as a projection of the masses, which would most certainly do the same things if the roles were changed.

Greed is a general thing, as is corruption and lust. Those at the top are equal to the ones at the bottom.

The level of sin that we witness today is shocking only to the ones who can't access such temptations. For the higher one goes in the social or financial hierarchy, the most tempted he will certainly be. It is only natural!

Even the most religious leaders can't deny the beauty of some or their followers, and consistently resist the sexual temptations provided by their senses.

This said, can we affirm that humans are temped to be evil?

I would say that humans are fundamentally neutral. Depends on what you do with them — the direction given by the environment.

Humans adapt to their surroundings. Many studies in psychology have shown that. Therefore, if we can control this environment — diet, education, and culture —, we can control, to a great extent, and even predict, the future of most people.

Another thing that we know, is that humans are guided by pleasure — sex, reputation, social recognition, etc. Therefore, the good and the bad depend on how this pleasure is controlled and channelled.

The environment is only as powerful as it is reinforced through its emotional channels. In this sense, someone who is unlucky in a bad environment, is more likely to succeed than that who is viewed as popular and attractive by that same environment.

That doesn't invalidate the existence of free will. A piece of fruit can be as tasty as a piece of chocolate. The first will be healthier than the second. And we can always choose one or the other.

Likewise, sex with love is healthier than sex without love. And yet, for most people, sex is a purely physical activity, because they cannot love. And this is why they cheat and abandon easily.

The less empathy there is in a person, the more likely this is to occur. Religious indoctrination and cultural values won't change this predisposition,

In fact, when the inner world of a person contradicts the external world, this individual will back-rationalize his or her own actions, in order to justify the manifestation of this nature on the outside. "He made me do it", "it is his fault", "I can't handle stress", "I have too much pressure", are just some of the phrases people tend to use to justify their own irrational actions. Most of which are against their own survival.

Misery is often a result of many bad and unconscious, even irresponsible, decisions in time. But few consider this, when making choices based on their instincts.

Chapter 10: How are We Controlled by Our Impulses?

Humans are emotional creatures and not truly rational. Reason always follows emotional perceptions. And so, to choose to say that people are evil or good is to be naive in both cases, if we don't consider this predisposition for pleasure.

Moreover, the more traumatic has been the past of a person, the more needy this person will be for love and affection.

Promiscuity is therefore a consequence of such traumas, and not normal. Praising promiscuity is as well part of this social sickness. The expansion of the sickness won't change its nature as such.

We can analyze this situation by observing how people are wired. For example, I can't be evil because I'm not wired that way, but that doesn't mean that I can't get angry and shout at someone. I do have empathy, therefore, I even regret feeling anger, but this sense of regret is part of a self-control mechanism within me, as anger is not part of my nature. Whenever I am constantly made angry in a relationship, I end it. And yet, most women, are so familiar with drama and conflict, that they actually get comfortable with it, and are surprised when such relationships come to an end.

Most people are too familiar with sickness to understand a healthy lifestyle. Happiness makes them nervous! That is why they lack basic self-control.

Now, why do I have it? Because I have the knowledge. I know too much, not to feel empathy.

Can we then say that evil comes from ignorance and the good comes from awareness?

Yes, we can say that. But it is more correct to say that, the more people understand the benefits of being good, the more they will want to be good.

If they see more benefits in being evil, they will choose to be evil.

This duality leads to great challenges in arguing with individuals who are predominantly evil. Because most evil people are actually protecting themselves from the evil of others.

Essentially, it is a justified evil. The psychopath, the narcissist, the sociopath, they are all trying to protect themselves and avoiding getting hurt. Even if their fear is delusional.

They are so immersed in their pain, that they can't leave their shelf, not even inside their relationships.

The problem is that, in the process, they become blind to the good people as well. Unless they can see them as an advantage for their own personal goals.

Such is indeed a dual paradox of the sick minds:

- They want to be loved but can't feel love;
- They don't believe in good people but fear bad people.

When a narcissist falls in love, not only will she choose someone who is kind, but will also think and express a belief that contradicts her perceptions, when saying:

— "You pretend to be someone you're not".

That is exactly what makes such individuals mentally ill. They doubt their own reality. Even though they are perfectly aware of what is good and bad. Otherwise, they wouldn't be such good liars.

Narcissists have mastered the art of fooling others, due to their exaggerated need to pretend to be someone they are not, in order to be accepted and admired. The reasons don't matter as much as the emotional fuel they get through this attention.

They then hurt the one whom they choose to trust because they believe that, if they do that, they won't be hurt back; and if they are not hurt back, they persist, because they can't believe they won't be hurt.

THE ANTICHRIST: THE GRAND PLAN OF TOTAL GLOBAL ENSLAVEMENT

Mankind is their enemy. And so, they have to justify their own belief-system. And which is, simultaneously, what makes them evil and what makes this topic so complex to analyze for the mental health community.

Many people who believe to be doing good, are actually doing much evil. And the leaders of social media are the best example of that.

Chapter 11: Why is Communism Evil?

Whenever someone pushes for socialist or communist ideologies on others, the result is always, as it has always been, a totalitarian abuse. And this is what the social media platforms have been practicing, by eliminating free speech, and manipulating their information, either related to the search results on the platform, or businesses being run online.

According to Dan Peña (2017), "Before Google changed the algorithms, they used to want 100 guys who produced a 100 million online. Now they want 10 million guys, who produce 10 thousand online. That is how they produced their platform".

The idea of giving equal opportunities to everyone, actually destroys the potential of anyone who can make these opportunities worthwhile.

The constant suppression of information, that is relevant for a realistic thinking, and the access to free information, also makes Google become just another totalitarian platform. And the same applies to Twitter, Pinterest, Facebook, Instagram, and so on. Because they follow the same beliefs and guidelines.

In a world controlled by computer geeks, people are just numbers. Capitalism, as in a free market, is not something they can understand.

In fact, from a mathematical point of view, communism makes much more sense to them. And it is more profitable too!

That is why, in China, the merging of technology with the totalitarian government, has been working so well — to equalize the nation at the same level of servitude, to catch dissents, to basically find and eliminate any opposition to this great machine, while enhancing its potential as a whole, e.g., empowering this beast furthermore. And that is evil!

Communism is always evil, but most people can't see it, precisely because Communism grows out of the collective need for a satisfaction of the sense of entitlement.

In other words, Communism only works in communities where the people are too selfish, too stupid and too evil, to grow in a social environment out of their own work and self-worth.

It would be like a plant asking a gardener to be scientifically engineered and grown in a greenhouse, because it cannot do it alone, or a bear asking to be put in a zoo because he can't catch fish and raise himself in the forest.

Are we transforming the whole planet into a big zoo or greenhouse because we hate freedom so much that we accept to be just numbers and statistics?

Most people like communism because they believe that, the entrepreneur who worked 16 hours a day for ten years, to build his own business, has the same value of the employee who works only because he has to, in order to pay for his rent and food.

Most employees don't even understand that, their salary is only possible, because the owner of the business worked hard enough to make it a reality. They don't understand that they are not entitled to that money, only the opportunity to work.

The employees work for the money, but they are paid because of their productivity, not the hours spent at the office.

The same problem of lack of understanding occurs with the many people I encounter, and who think I am 'lucky', and that the only reason why I make so much money, is because I fool others into paying for what I write. Some actually got very angry — and in one case, she even spilled a beer on me — after I said I don't believe in advertising books.

They think I am hiding some secret, when I explain that value is self-evident. They think I am insulting when talking about value because they have none.

Chapter 12: Why is Money Not Evil?

When you say to someone, "You should make money out of value", they understand it as, "You have no value", because the same sentence reflects back at them their real worth — as an individual behind the mask they portray to others.

That is why you offend with the truth. People don't want the truth! They want validation to their lies and illusions instead.

That is why the most sold books, have nothing to do with their content's value, but everything to do with their titles. Titles that contain sentences like, "fuck-it" and "not giving a fuck", are appealing to the masses, because they match their selfish views on reality. To call them spiritual or self-help manuals, is to literally mock the incapacity of these same buyers to self-reflect. It is like projecting an image without explaining its source.

You see, everyone enjoys watching movies, but nobody really knows and nobody cares about how a television exactly works or why it works, or how a computer projects a movie on the screen. You don't have to know how to build a TV or a computer to watch a movie. You also don't have to know why electricity is real to become an electrician.

This analogy, however, expands to the fundamental fact, that people also don't question the motives behind the news they watch and the information they receive.

The perception can't be reached because they have not surpassed their own need for an egotistic validity — which is constantly fed, through a push and pull mechanism used in what is transmitted on the screen. It is the rule of "I give you this, if you feel the need for that".

There is, indeed, an exchange occurring, when we watch a movie or the news. But this exchange is subliminal, as in an hypnotic state. The individual is giving away his rights to his own mind, in exchange for the emotions received.

This is why Hollywood focuses so much on the visual aspect of its movies but little on the content. The content is nothing but a complete brainwashing of the dumb masses, mesmerized and hypnotized with lasers, explosions, violence, murder and blood.

Your emotions are not bad. It is what you do with them that is — as when allowing them to manipulate your thinking process.

Likewise, money is also neither good or bad. It is how you use it that makes it good or bad — for you can use money to get fat and buy junk to impress others, or to invest on your own health and future. A future in which you become more independent from the governments and the social structure, and even your country.

Nobody wants that! Nobody even wants to think about that!

Chapter 13: Why are People Mentally Enslaved?

The fact that most people are mentally enslaved, becomes obvious when I tell them that I can live where I want and change country whenever I want, and they think I am a criminal. This level of freedom, to be anywhere in the world, and at any moment, based on nothing but a personal decision — a singularity detached from the implications, mechanisms, regulations and reinforcements of the environment — is so surreal to the vast majority, that they consider it to be illegal.

Isn't this funny? When you are able to break free from the reality in which everyone is imprisoned, they think you are, somehow, an outlaw. Because their reality is their law. They can't dissociate reality from law.

Law is based on moral, and so, if you can control the paradigms of belief of the masses, you will also control their reality — the social perceptions of it, along with its mechanics and regulations. In doing so, you control moral and law simultaneously.

Mayer Amschel Rothschild said: "Permit me to issue and control the money of a nation, and I care not who makes its laws". And the same principle applies, if someone says: "Give me power over the belief system of the masses, and I care not who makes their reality."

Looking at myself as an example of what I just said, we can ask: Who am I in this reality? A writer?

No, I am not a writer. That is the how I am viewed. Behind the illusion of reality, I am actually a God's sparkle trying to create a fire.

Jesus said: "Do not think that I came to bring peace on the Earth. I did not come to bring peace, but a sword" (Matthew 10:34). This sword was a metaphor to the truth that had to cut through the lies for the soul to emerge as an independent thinking individual. And that is why I tell you that I came here to bring fire.

I am, however, just one of the many sparkles of fire on this planet, trying to burn the system to the ground, for the truth to emerge.

Why fire? Because a sword can't cut through anymore. This system of lies is now too interconnected and entangled with the soul, the mind and the body, as well as the physical reality, to allow spiritual freedom to manifest itself independently.

Chapter 14: The War on Awareness.

The war we have now is on awareness, and that is why I had to become a writer. I believe many others doing my work, are doing it through other bridges, that allow to break free through the same fire — awakening.

According to the world we have today, this fire has to be produced through the many bridges of communication — art, public speaking, books, fiction, music, etc.

If you want to find the sparkles of God, you must search for them through these means of awakening.

Could religion be one of such means?

It was in the past, but not anymore.

Religions have bended to the type of control described here and became corrupted. All of them.

That is why, even the most dedicated to their religion, seem too stupid and too selfish. That is why even love is meaningless in such world.

The religious ones tend to contradict their own books, and become unable to understand them, because their brain is incapable of dissociating from the beliefs of the outside world. And the ones who love, can only love within these patterns as well. Reason why people are now so materialistic and superficial in their relationships and choice of partners.

As such, the Freemasons, the Rosicrucians, the Christians, the Hindus, the Muslims, the Buddhists, they all think I am too awaken to be real, too smart to be normal, too enlightened to be enlightened, to able to be unable under their beliefs, to independent to fit their group. And that scares them, and makes them imagine all kinds of perversities, among which, the most logic for them, fits the criteria to exclude me from their life, and in doing so, their own reality — either it is to believe that I am possessed by powerful demons (as with christians), or that I belong to a Secret Religious Organization they never heard about, as is the case with all the Secret Societies I encounter, e.g., an Organization so secret that even the secret ones never heard about.

Now, imagine if I could read their minds too and exercise my telepathic rights? What would happen?

I tell you what happens! They get scared even more, and say that I am possessed by Satan himself. Because now, not only have I broken the laws of the system, but also broken into the laws of what they consider to be possible for a human being.

Many even believe that I am trying to create a religion that will destroy theirs. And wouldn't that be the cherish on top of the cake? Because that fear reflects what must actually happen to their religion.

You can expect all kinds of psychopathic reactions when moving out of the reality of the majority, because this majority is so immersed in their own illusions, that they won't see they are in a jail.

That is probably the greatest trick ever pulled on humanity — to make people believe that their prison is the new normal.

In fact, the sentence "new normal", has been used often by the different news channels from around the world, during the COVID-19 pandemic, as a way of brainwashing the population into accepting lockdowns and monitoring devices as a new way of living.

Chapter 15: How Beliefs Keep People Poor and Stupid.

You can't ask a person, who has never understood herself, to understand how the world works. You can't ask someone, who has never done anything of value in her life, to see that others only want that same, still inexistent, value.

The two realities are incompatible because the individual can't bridge them. If she could, she would not have the problems she has. As such, people bridge the misunderstandings with the illusions they receive, because those illusions are more reachable.

Preparing a salad takes time. Frying a stake is fast. Being a vegan then consumes too much work, which means having a healthy diet consumes more energy. And people don't want the difficult path. They want the easiest one! They want to be able to just boil some potatoes or pasta, sprinkle some seeds on the top, and call themselves vegan. And, in the same way, they want to come out with a magical idea that makes them rich, while offering zero value to the rest of the planet.

That is why, the more self-absorbed and ignorant people are, the more power the government has. The two things are proportional to one another and related. As such, people are made stupid, through the chemicals in the water, the toxins in their vaccines and chemtrails in the air, and even their own education, in order to push them as downwards as possible.

What these same leaders can't see, is that, with the suppression of society, they go along with it — downwards.

They then have to keep on suppressing society at the same pace that they themselves are suppressed, for they keep on being as stupid as the rest.

It is the selfish mindset that keeps them from self-reflecting through their observations — looking at the mirror they form. But narcissists and psychopaths have to do what narcissists and psychopaths do.

As soon as people understand that we are all interconnected, and can actually see this, what I am saying becomes self-evident.

On the another hand, it is precisely because the majority has this selfish pro-communist mindset, that they allow companies and leaders with the same goals and beliefs to gain power and prosper. The leadership of the masses has to reflect the mindset of these masses.

However, the prosperity of the communist-orientated companies and governments, comes with a high cost to those who are truly moving society forward. The communist attempts of Google and Amazon to democratize authors' earnings, is what destroyed my own earnings almost entirely. I lost more than 90% of what I was getting in book sales because they pushed all of my books backwards into the depths of the search engines. And this, to equalize earning opportunities among authors. Otherwise, as a business model, their online book selling system would collapse. Because, you see, I was among the top 1% of authors, making more than 90% of all the rest combined.

This statistical fact, that many consider to be evil, is actually a reflection of the type of world in which we live and has nothing of evil in it.

As a University Professor, I saw this statistical rule applying all the time, in front of my eyes. Whenever I explained something very important, 1% of the students, or that is, one in every one hundred, would copy my information, ask me questions and apply it, while the rest would systematically be looking at their mobiles, waiting for when was time to leave the classroom. They were systematically bored. So bored, that anything and everything made them bored. They only valued entertainment.

One of the most difficult classes I ever gave them, was actually when I tried to explain the difference between entertainment and education. They were too brainwashed to understand.

Chapter 16: Capitalism is a Luxury of the Smartest!

I once got a complain from a group of students, who said to the Directors of the University, that I had wasted 3 hours — two classes, teaching how to start a business, instead of focusing on teaching how to create a curriculum and find a job.

I did teach both topics. I simply did not want to waste so much time on something that I consider to be of an inferior importance, and waste my knowledge on that, rather than teaching and resuming what I know about business in a short period of time.

Well, one student saw that, and took one hour to ask me questions. She was the only one among nearly two hundred students. One year later, she started a business of her own, following the model I gave her. A business that made her rich and allowed her to then employ some of her own colleagues. She used that money earned, to invest in another business, and start her own coffee shop brand. Now she has two businesses!

The rest of the students, later asked me what have I told her.

I answered them: "I told her the exact same things that I was saying to everyone else. But everyone complained about it, and even asked the other teachers to stop me."

It is then obvious that, in a Communist or Socialist orientated world, in which social media is guided towards what the majority wants, the choices that people make, in what they want to read or learn, are irrelevant, for both the information and the access to it can be manipulated, if the majority is too stupid to think and see what they truly need and is good their future.

The need to fit in is the cause of such massive stupidity!

You can't want what you can't see. And if what you want is conditioned by others, then you won't ever know what you truly, as an individual, want. The need to fit in distorts that perception.

The truth is that, if a teacher can't or won't teach you how to start your own business, the opportunity is simply not available to you within the educational system.

The idea that you are free is then segregated to the collective imaginary of possibilities that are not truly there.

If knowing how to create your own CV is all you get, that is truly all you will know.

Stupidity is then, at the college level, a consequence of the accumulation of useless, or conditioned, information, rather than the lack of it.

Most of the college graduates are filled with arrogance, but are as stupid as when they started studying for their degree.

They were conditioned to believe and protect the system as a religion, in order to replicate this same system without questioning it. Their delusional view of themselves emerges from this deceptive knowing.

Chapter 17: Stupidity is a Contagious Disease!

Only those who have never wrote more than a 100 books in their life, think that stupidity is not a contagious disease and the most destructive of them all.

In truth, it is better to live a good life with a properly working brain, capable of effective decisions, than an entire life as a moron. But the stupid will never understand this. And it is obvious that they are a majority. As such, the world will always be a difficult place for those who want to write 100 books.

If you try to write 300, or 500, then the planet will seem like a hell full of demons and psychopaths walking around mad — a zombie apocalypse full of retarded morons trying to eat you and drink your blood.

That is exactly how the world feels to someone who is trying to evolve beyond common standards.

When the common standards lower, you can't help but to get angry all the time. Unless you lower your own standards too.

The stupid, dumb and moronic ones, will say that ignorance is bliss, because they believe in this lowering of one's standards to fit in.

It is then no surprise that they tend to defend socialism and communism. Because the fat always love the cake. The who things, dumb ideas and stupidity, have to combine together, or logic wouldn't exist. But what is logic for the one who can't possibly comprehend the vastness of the implications of his own actions? Who can't possibly understand how one person can change the world?

They never wrote 100 books, or 50, or even one in most cases. They have no idea of what it means to change anything, much less the world. They are happier in accepting the world as it is. And they will call that state 'happiness'.

I would say that, if they put a gun to their head and pull the trigger, the reality they will face, when seeing their dead body on the ground, won't be that different as the one they have now.

Anyone who defends mass mandatory anything, either it is a vaccine, a common belief, or quite simply, a merging with a downgrading system, is an enemy to mankind as much as he is to himself.

The false prophets are out there, for anyone to see — they tell you to just be happy and accept life as it is, and enjoy being a disgusting human being; they will tell you that, even in the worse case scenario, you can just be happy and meditate; as if the lack of responsibility that put you in that scenario in the first place, shouldn't be taken into consideration.

The morons love them, because as I said, the fat has to love the cake.

The stupid will always worship, praise and admire, even promote, the stupid. And that is how you know someone is very stupid.

As soon as someone tells me I should read Eckhart Tolle, or some other stupid moron, I immediately know I have an idiot in front of me. And such is the case, as they themselves prove in time.

What does it mean to give them equal opportunities, and the chance to prove themselves and explain themselves?

It means to deny myself the responsibility to avoid stupidity. As then I get contaminated, and my body fights it back, with anger and frustration. Because anger is what you feel when your body is trying to fight off the disease of stupidity.

The majority don't understand this! They are too stupid and brainwashed to see it!

When they have a fever, they take a pill to lower the temperature, not knowing that the temperature rises to eliminate the toxins that cause that fever. A fever is actually how the body eliminates cancerous cells and dangerous toxins.

They also don't know that sweating is how they lower their weight. They want to eat the cake and be slim without working for the perfect body. It doesn't work that way! And yet, they are shocked with the results.

THE ANTICHRIST: THE GRAND PLAN OF TOTAL GLOBAL ENSLAVEMENT

The same with being smart. You can't be smart and not react to stupidity. You can't just take a pill of happiness, or pretend the disease of ignorance is not contaminating you.

Nobody will ever be smart and happy all the time! That illusion, in which the morons want to believe, keeps them poor. But then they will think that life is unfair, because they have many friends and that should be equivalent to wealth, as if popularity and wealth were correlated. Many actually believe it is!

Many people tell me that if I was more popular, I would be richer. And that is why they are poor.

You see, whenever you equalize everything, as in 'fat eats cake and fat gets rich, and fat can be stupid and rich and slim, and lies can be truths', not only are you heading downwards, to the abyss of ultimate ignorance, but you are also heading yourself towards a very dangerous reality, a kind of special hell.

In submerging yourself to such an illusion of absolute equality, then aided by painkillers and drugs, that becomes the only world in which you can continue on living, and if you wish to call that a life.

Then these people wonder: What is the purpose of life?

It starts with actually having one.

Chapter 18: Being Dumb is a Choice!

Most people don't understand that the choices they make condition the opportunities they get and type of society they get. As such, the current social media companies — like Facebook, Google, Twitter, Instagram, Pinterest, and so on — by manipulating their search engines and their listings, in order to please the masses, not only kill the success of an author with the simplicity of a decision, but also create a social damage for many years to come, and beyond the capacity we have to analyze it in a short period of time.

Their algorithms and their censorship, and basically, all the decisions they make, affect us all. And if Mark Zuckerberg is a nazi, then Facebook is a dictatorship. And Mark Zuckerberg is indeed a nazi. But nazi censorship through facebook is now so normal, people won't even protest. They are too afraid to be disconnected from their platforms filled with narcissistic photos.

Some people, are so financially dependent on the social media platforms, that they can't pay their rent if their page goes down. And yet, their greatest skill is often and just to simply take photos of their own body.

We now reward pornography and eroticism more than we reward knowledge. Which means society has redirected itself backwards, further towards its instincts.

Meanwhile, those who control most of the knowledge available today, such as Google and Amazon, consistently and systematically, downgrade the success of any author.

Personally, I went from being one of the most popular authors in the world, to becoming a common one in just a few months. They can and do just that by equalizing opportunities to gain the attention and acceptance of the majority.

Most authors feel entitled even though they are useless. Every single author I met to this day, asked me questions about how to sell more copies, but none asked me how to improve his own content or write better, or even write something that is valuable for other people.

They are ignorant, entitled and selfish! And readers can see it, reason why they can't sell books. However, the book businesses on social media can't grow, unless they grab the attention of the foolish majority. And that is why the good books are pushed backwards.

I still manage to sell thousands of books every month, but I have to go through many tactics to accomplish that, most of which have nothing to do with the content, but rather my background experience as a business owner and business consultant.

It is funny when some people I know say "Congratulations on your recent best seller", because they are unaware that I have reached the best selling charts nearly two hundred times already. I am simply putting this fact in the cover of my books now, for the first time. Because the majority is too dumb to notice such things, and social media won't show them either.

Chapter 19: The War on Information!

In the current world, the war is made with information. And I can only win because I can see the battlefield in front of me. But this is a constant war, with no end.

The majority is not even aware that there is a war going on. They are subject to the winds of change, and completely unconscious to how those changes occur.

They are too stupid to understand and too selfish to care.

On the other hand, and contrary to this vast majority, I don't believe in the possibility of achieving success because the masses know what quality is, or even in being altruistic, because the masses recognize good actions, or in selling many books because the masses will persist in finding the information needed, even if they have to go through all the books in the world.

I know well that this is all an illusion, in which many insist on believing, and will certainly keep them poor.

To be wealthy in today's world, you have to think like a warrior. Not because warriors are better than priests, or any other worker, but because, if the world is in a constant psychological war, only a warrior can handle such emotional and mental pressure.

It is not a coincidence that the most successful entrepreneurs have either been in the military or the martial arts.

If the information you need keeps being hidden from you, if the majority of the people you know are brainwashed and stupid, if there is a tremendous pressure to change you downwards and towards failure, and to make you feel isolated and segregated for thinking differently, then your only option is to accept this war with the mindset of a warrior.

The alternative will most likely lead you to depression, isolation and suicide. And that is why, those who are bullied and ostracized by society, or lose their marriage, tend to join the suicide statistics. They lack the fundamental training to handle psychological and emotional warfare.

You see, the Devil now moves through this social indoctrination and manipulation, and this is how he wins souls — by weakening, creating the fear of isolation, and by hiding the information from you.

Stupidity is indeed a choice in today's world, but not an easy choice.

The cost of following the truth, has led me to abandon many friends and relationships. You don't really have any other option, if you want the truth, because most people want the lie.

As it is said in the movie, the Matrix — through the character of Morpheus —, "Most people are not ready to be unplugged, and many of them are so inured and so hopelessly dependent on the system, that they will fight to protect it."

Fighting, in this case, means that they will choose to keep their jealous friends, their superficial relationships and the illusion that they have a respectful job, because they are too afraid to lose all of that.

They are, essentially, afraid to be stuck in happiness without friends. They rather have companionship in their misery, than loneliness in their happiness.

Heaven is empty because most soul choose to socialize in hell.

Chapter 20: Can We Be Kind to Others?

Despite the conditions presented to us in this world, we can choose to be kind. You can be kind! But not before you are willing to see tears and blood in the battlefield of life.

I had to let go thousands of friendships, face ridicule multiple times, and end dozens of relationships with women I loved, to achieve my goals. And I have no regrets, because my values are high. But I can't say that, even the memories, don't cause me a tremendous pain and many sleepless nights.

I also can't say that I expect others to be able to face the same level of pain.

Emotional pain can be hard to endure and as much as physical pain.

If I am still succeeding, after so many years passed, it is only because the ones who love what they read, those who trust my words, buy everything I produce, and share it with their friends. I am basically winning by worth of mouth — recognized value.

This success has nothing to do with Amazon or Google, or any other of the many devilish, socialistic and wicked companies out there.

Those — communist ideology followers — manipulate sales and manipulate their rankings, while manipulating social opinion.

In such an empire of devilish communists, I am just a small monarch amidst gigantic warlords. A rebel! And indeed, that is how most people see me — an outcast.

As being self-sufficient and oppose the system is now as rare as finding a dinosaur, most people can't even believe I am real. The vast majority of the people I have encountered, more than 95% of them, don't believe I am a full-time author, and much less a well-paid author.

Most of the women I met actually told me: "I think you should find a normal job."

They can't understand that I make more money than they do while I sleep.

Nevertheless, historically, we have seen what happens when greed rules over the masses. And that is why most people read useless literature. The shittiest books are always pushed to the top of the lists. And most people are too lazy to search. That requires too much work from their lazy mind.

In todays' world, to be lazy, and refuse to question and to distrust what is offered, is so common, that the masses won't even self-analyze the consequences of such habit.

My readers are and have to be — due to what I have explained before, — completely different from this majority. And indeed, they constantly tell me that they have to read a lot, before they can finally find my books. Then, they send me messages saying: "I have read so much crap for the past years, that I never though I could even find the truth anymore, the real truth as expressed in your books. I was losing hope and never thought I could ever find this truth."

This truth, that they are mentioning, is now so scarce, that I can create new pen-names and get the exact same replies, either it is for books related to spirituality, religion, psychology, general self-help, or even novels and fiction.

This war that we face today, is a war to which the vast majority is not ready. It implies the ability to confront reality at many levels, within our mind, spirit and emotions. And most are simply not ready for that. They don't possess the weapons to win.

In its origins, as in its manifestations, we notice that it is a war between light and darkness. Let us not be fooled about it! It is a war between wisdom and ignorance!

The dark ages are today ruled by mass ignorance, and as such, to a great extent, we are still in the dark ages.

In today's world, anyone who starts from the bottom, is facing a war of David against Goliat. And that is why I insist that one must believe in God and have faith, as there is no other way to win.

THE ANTICHRIST: THE GRAND PLAN OF TOTAL GLOBAL ENSLAVEMENT

One must persist and be consistent with his own values and faith in order to win. At least, in his life, as the majority of the population is lost already.

Chapter 21: Why are Most People So Ignorant?

What we consider to be a reality is in fact a combination of values, emotions and ideas, promoted through different sources, and leading us to filter the truth according to a network of principles.

Such world is not the real world, but the world we are told to believe, the world built for us to follow. Because when the majority agrees with a lie, then that lie becomes a truth — and that truth becomes their reality.

This is easier to apply in a large scale than many would imagine. And as an example, we can see the country with the highest population number in the world — China — still believing that Mao Zedong was a great leader, completely ignoring that he killed more Chinese than any other dictator before him.

It is with the same strategy in mind, that the first catholics changed the word Elohim in the gnostic writings — meaning Gods — to God as a singular individual.

More amazing than the biggest lies in the world, are the rejected truths, and that those, deep inside this manipulation, cannot even confront, and would rather violently oppose.

When the Nag Hammadi library was found, christians from around the world closed their eyes and turned their faces away from that truth. Which was far distant from the lies of the Vatican and other religious organizations in which they've chosen to believe. Despite the fact that all biblical versions are translations from the same Catholic book.

These christians still choose to follow their own religious movements, rejecting this or any other truth being found, because they are afraid of what changing implies. And it is precisely this fear of change — the unknown — that keeps people stuck to their stupidity, immersed in a complete ignorance.

Many followers of different religions claim to follow the truth, and yet, they fear the truth. They refuse to accept the fact that they live a lie, even when the truth is brought forward to their world. The beliefs of the group become superior to the truth. And their God is in fact the god of the group — a delusional belief shared by everyone.

This state of mind then allows for manipulation to occur easily. For most people rather believe a lie inside a group than a truth by themselves.

There are billions of people in the world, living within the same structured perspective of reality. And they are all too afraid to awake. So afraid, that they violently attack, usually with spiteful words, anyone pointing at their open wounds.

They are like walking-dead on Earth; the dead souls that the bible talks about. For they are the ones who will never resurrect from the dead.

On the other hand, in the world we know today, the search for the truth isolates the wisest, strips them from their own dignity, and condemns them to a path of disrespect and constant ridicule by society as a whole.

The real christians are still being crucified for loving the truth.

The ones who live within the norms, see themselves as superior to those outside of them, like little children that have never grown up. They think that, if they follow the rules, they are behaving just as good little girls and good little boys. And thanks to their parents, they have in their brain the idea that obeying leads to rewards and not obeying to punishment.

This is why most people subconsciously believe that, if a person loses the job, divorces or gets a disease, it is because he or she has done something bad to deserve it.

Moreover, they will avoid such people, because that is also how they were raised when watching cartoons: good guys can't hangout with bad guys.

THE ANTICHRIST: THE GRAND PLAN OF TOTAL GLOBAL ENSLAVEMENT

People are indoctrinated in a vast amount of ways, and then try to justify their imbecility, because they have, at one point, become too stupid to look at themselves in the mirror and admit how ignorant they truly are.

Most of them rather continue in the same path of lies. It is easier than to rethink their whole existence.

Chapter 22: Can Humans Be Enslaved?

The global agenda, with the intention of transforming human beings, in any way possible, into obeying machines, is so well-built, that matches perfectly into what is already believed inside the educational system, popular religions, and even within what is promoted by mainstream science.

Any attempt at moving apart from this agenda, is faced with social segregation and condemned in many ways, even by force, and with the use of the law if necessary.

Alan Dershowitz — Professor at Harvard Law School — explained in an interview to Crowdsource (2020), that "You have no right not to be vaccinated, you have no right not to wear a mask, you have no right to open up your business... and if you refuse to be vaccinated, the state has the power to literally take you to a doctor's office and plunge a needle into your arm... if the vaccination is designed to prevent a spreading disease."

According to Dershowitz, under democratic law, a person only owns the right to die. He said that, "If the vaccination is only to prevent a disease that you will get, that will kill you, you have the right to refuse that. But you have no right to refuse to be vaccinated against a contagious disease. The police have the power of the Constitution, that gives the state the power, to compel that in the United States".

What this means is that, in the United States, as in any other democratic nation, the government has the right to inject people with whatever is under the law, and even force that vaccination with the use of the police.

The law, literally gives the right for the police to break into someone's home and inject anything into this person by force.

Moreover, anyone who refuses such actions, will be acting against the law — will be a criminal.

Even though this seems like the scene of an apocalyptical science fiction movie, it is within the realms of possibility in democratic nations. Dershowitz says, "That is what a democracy is about. If the majority of the people agree and support this public health measures, you have to be vaccinated. If you want to interact with other people, the constitution doesn't give you the right to spread your illness to other people".

In short, the government has the right to inject drugs, toxins and nanorobotics into people's body. And, according to Dershowitz, "You can disagree, you can be a dissenter, you can leave the country, but what you can't do, is say 'I don't agree, therefore I am going to take the law into my own hands'. That is not a constitutional right... We are talking about democracy. The decision is made by the government through democratic means."

Dershowitz continues on saying that he "Would like to see government mandated vaccine... and will defend it."

Most people actually believe in the stupid logic, that a mandated vaccine is the only way to protect society from a disease, as if there was logic in the fact that the vaccination of some won't work unless everyone else is vaccinated.

That is like saying that a certain cure won't work, unless everyone else takes the same medicine.

It is stupid! Dershowitz is stupid! And the fact that we have professors of law and governments defending this stupidity, shows us that democracy doesn't work. If the majority is stupid, democracy becomes the law of the stupid!

Chapter 23: Why Do People Agree with a Dumb Logic?

The reason why people agree with dumb logic has a lot to do with their ignorance. But much truth has been suppressed already. And so, the world continues in a spiritual slavery, not knowing how far everyone is from the true reality being hidden below the surface.

Within the current reality, the masses can see only who is creating the rules and who is following them, noticing how fate is merely a consequence of those who change such laws. And so, lies are taken as truths, and become mainstream when fulfilling corporative goals.

Each person has now inside the brain a program of what reality is and can be. These strong beliefs tell them that they are right, simply because they follow a majority and fit into what the media tells them to do. And the need of being accepted and belonging to society, leads them into this mass schizophrenia without any consideration for any other possibility.

If people could see reality with their spirit instead of their mind, they could step outside the paradigms and learn more, but the vast majority can't do that anymore. They have forgotten their spiritual nature.

When taking a closer look at what are the left and right side of the brain doing, we can notice that social paradigms enforce an imprisoning of humans inside the left side. This part of the brain tells us that reality is what we see. Therefore, people see what is logic, even though this logic has been programmed by someone in the social hierarchy in which they experience reality.

It is with the right side that you transform logic with creativity — the analysis of new possibilities. But most end up living a social life with the left-brain. Or, in other words, in a world of those who create the rules and those who obey them.

The right-brain thinkers — commonly, the creative ones and the conspiracists — are often seen as crazy or extravagant, because they are a minority in a world of imbeciles.

The social system we know today, ridicules, mocks and despises the ones operating mostly with the right side of the brain — artists and independent spiritual thinkers —, and while passing the subliminal message that, if you want to survive in the 'real world', you must get out of the right brain viewpoint.

This is where the first false belief starts — the 'if I am right, others must be wrong', for it creates the illusion of division in society.

Beyond this belief, comes the indifference towards those suffering, the beggars and the unemployed or, mores simply, the tendency to avoid those who somehow suffer with social issues and different types of problems.

These individuals represent the overall decreasing in awareness, empathy and compassion.

The more people isolate themselves behind computer screens and other electronic devices, the more indifferent they become as well. As social networks and the need to please others exist now as a way to replace what should be a normal interaction between human beings.

Chapter 24: The Neo-Anarchists.

The new form of opposition in the era of technology, or anarchism — as in a protest against authority — comes as a complete isolation. For the individual now feels that he or she is, one way or another, persuaded from all corners of society and always discriminated, either it is for being an atheist, a religious person, a man, a woman, or basically, a defender of his or her own rights in what concerns being free and happy.

Freedom is truly an illusion, when the vast majority of society discriminates you for being, looking or acting different.

The Elite succeeded in dividing society and turning it against itself. For if in the past being an anarchist meant opposing the government, it now means to oppose democracy — the sheeple mentality.

One would assume that after many centuries of wars between nations, and with the creation of the European union, which allowed many poor countries, such as Poland, Estonia, Lithuania, or Latvia, to recover in a short period of time, Europe would be more united, and yet, xenophobia is still very present in most states, and especially, in these ones. But why are people so stupid, and ignorant, despite everything that they obviously get, when being more open-minded to tourism and other nations from around the world?

Saudi Arabia, for example, is among the richest countries in the world, and close to 40% of their population is composed by foreigners.

We can assume that the media, the government, and the Educational System, or the lack of proper education, of the general population, is the root cause behind such retrograde behaviors. But the overall manipulation of the will of the public, one way or another, does happen through advertising, music, the media, the news, and so on.

The individual is left today with his or her own mind under attack at every single moment of the day and wherever he or she goes. To be a rebel in today's world is, basically, to be able to think.

The Neo-anarchists are AnarchoRationalists — those who do not conform with the laws, because they are better informed than the majority.

On the other hand, this attack on the freedom to think, leads us to the importance of what some of the most popular anarchists and libertarians warned, namely, Emma Goldman. She said that, "Anarchism stands for liberation of the human mind from the dominion of religion, the liberation of the human body from the dominion of property, liberation from shackles and restraint of government. It stands for social order based on the free grouping of individuals."

This type of freedom is now barely valued. For what once was represented as the freedom from governmental oppression, is now a freedom that shows itself necessary at a very personal and mental level — the freedom to be able to think and decide independently, while risking losing the companionship and friendship of others.

This new type of freedom comes with a very high price. It costs us our own socialization.

It is for this reason noticeable, in particular, the situation of many women who decide to embrace the traditional values, of having a family, and being a stay-at-home-mum, as they are verbally bullied by others, even on social media, including other women. And while men who want to educate society on the rights of men, get their videos, podcasts and books, systemically removed from the market and the media, and are violently censored by the general public.

Traditionalism, or even the right to protect values with thousands of years, is now under attack, because it goes against the general agenda. But is it a good agenda?

According to Dr. Dennis L. Cuddy, "The General Education Board (GEB), established by John D. Rockefeller, and chartered in 1902, was an effort toward the 'Goal of social control'. This goal was publicly mentioned in 1933, by Max Mason — President of the Rockefeller Foundation —, who assured trustees that, in their program "The Social Sciences will concern themselves with the rationalization of social control... the control of human behavior".

THE ANTICHRIST: THE GRAND PLAN OF TOTAL GLOBAL ENSLAVEMENT

Then, in the late 1950s, the National Mental Health Institute commenced a program to have public schools administer Ritalin to children classified as "dull" or "emotionally disturbed"". And that was only the beginning of a global war against individualism. For, in 1973, the Trilateral Commission was founded by David Rockfeller, with an agenda clearly stated by Zbigniew Brzezinski — the first director —, who wrote that there is "The increasing availability of biochemical means of human control... as human beings become increasingly manipulable and malleable".

The ultimate intention of this manipulation is the elimination of any form of identification — gender, family, religion, or patriotism, in any way possible. The individual is to come to a state in which he or she will doubt personal thoughts, then allowing a total control over the mind.

Chapter 25: The Use of Psychology Against The People.

Modern psychology would have to become part of the war on people's capability to think for themselves — including the religious thinking and beliefs — while psychologists and psychiatrists were molded to be used as moronic puppets of the system for mass indoctrination.

This conspiracy in the mental health community was exposed by Dr. Tana Dineen, a licensed psychologist who abandoned her clinical practice and wrote a book titled "Manufacturing Victims".

She said that, "Over ten million Americans seek the services of the Psychology Industry each year. In the early 1960's, 14% of the U.S. population (25 million of a total 180 million) had ever received psychological services. By 1976, that number had risen to 26%. However by 1990, at least 33% (65 million of 250 million) have been psychological users at some point in their lives and in 1995, the American Psychological Association stated that 46% of the U.S. population (128 million) had seen a mental health professional. Some even predict that by the year 2000 users will be the majority — constituting 80% of the population.

No longer can clear distinctions be made between psychology, psychiatry, psychoanalysis and clinical social work, as well as psychotherapy. With degrees in psychology, medicine, social work, nursing or with no academic qualifications at all, the expanding work force of the Psychology Industry relies for its survival and growth on its ability to manufacture victims.

The Psychology Industry can neither reform itself from within nor should it be allowed to try. It should be stopped from doing what it is doing to people, from manufacturing victims. And while the Psychology Industry is being dismantled, people can boycott psychological treatment, protest the influence of the Psychology Industry and resist being manufactured into victims."

The manufacture of victims is based on the idea that anyone can be labeled unbalanced for a multitude of reasons, and therefore subject to an arbitrary diagnostic that will inevitably categorize the individual with some sort of disorder, allowing then the means for law enforcement of treatment or mandatory psychotropic medication, imposed by governments.

The stages in which this control over the masses occurs, was outlined by F.E. Emery in the book 'Futures We Are In':

- The first stage is when people "lose their moral judgment" or sense of personal identification;

- The second stage is a "segmentation" or societal disintegration and discrimination, in which the individual's attention moves towards a preoccupation with the local community or family;

- The third and last stage is dissociation: "A world in which fantasy and reality are indistinguishable," leading the individual to become merely a part of the societal unit and identified only in this way.

Emery says that, this final result, replaces random violence and protest with a retreat to television sets and other forms of "virtual reality" — communication and social interactions would be made exclusively through mobiles and computers.

The new ideal individual would then, as we see today, become an antisocial being, living under the illusion that he or she is being social — by interacting through a virtual world designed to reprogram, indoctrinate and enslave.

Anyone who doesn't assimilate to this absurd way of living, is labeled as "crazy", insane, and then discriminated, first by society, and then by the Mental Health Industry, which will see him or her as someone that "doesn't fit in" and needs to be reprogrammed, drugged and put back into the social pool.

Chapter 26: The Eradication of the Individuality.

Many of the values being promoted today, namely, through the propaganda of socialism and globalism, intend to actually promote a dissociation between the individual and his or her own cultural identity, which will inevitably lead to a weaker personality, then sought to be found through the identity of a group.

Dr. Ewen Cameron — former President of the American Psychiatric Association — explained that, "When the technique has been perfected, every government that has been in charge of education for a generation, will be able to control its subjects securely without the need of armies or policemen... Educational propaganda, with government help, could achieve this result in a generation.

There are, however, two powerful forces opposed to such a policy: one is religion; the other is nationalism... A scientific world society cannot be stable unless there is a world government."

This statement, tells us that, there is the intention of making people so obedient to their governments, that they will police each other and report each other, as what we see happening in Communist countries. But for this to occur, the sense of identity must be eliminated. For people cannot have any other system of values apart from those imposed by the government.

As such, religion and nationalism, become natural oppositions that must be destroyed, or at least, controlled to such an extent that, a difference between government and religion or nationalism, can't be perceived any longer.

This separation of the individual from his sense of gender, nationality and religion, then necessarily leads this individual to a greater co-dependency between him and the government.

This is also what we have been witnessing over the past decades, as religions and nationalists seem to replicate, in a way or another, the exact same values of the new world government, and while the Educational System insists on the promotion of atheism and the subversion of religious beliefs — which are both ridiculed and discredited.

At a subconscious level, different behavior modifications are then expected from the individual:

- Obey the hierarchy and ignore your own personal judgement;

- The moral of the group is superior to the ethical code of the individual;

- Any dissident, is either to be discredited, ridiculed, changed or expelled.

As you may have noticed, this practice is common in many Religious Congregations, as much as it is common inside the Educational System, and in particular, in many Universities throughout the world.

Chapter 27: The Corruption of the Religious Faith.

The elimination of the religions of the world as they were, was parallel with the plan of controlling education.

A tight control at the top of the hierarchy, would guarantee that any religious group in existence, would have to be — as with the educational system — aligned with the goals of the Power Elite.

A technique to eliminate religious influence in the society, was mentioned by Edgar C. Bundy, (In Collectivism in the Church, 1958), when saying that, "Because 'mental health' has become available as a lever to be used for promoting political and ideological designs, a word on the subject is in order... People who are normal in every sense of the word but who hold unpopular political ideas, such as opposition to world government and to the United Nations, Federal aid to education, and socialism, are now being branded by their opponents as 'lunatics,' 'nuts' and 'idiots'. Some of the mental health legislation which has been recently introduced on the state and Federal levels gives such wide latitude of interpretations to psychiatrists and politicians... that it is conceivable that anyone who takes a stand for the sovereignty of the United States, in favor of Congressional investigations... and in favor of states' rights could be committed to an asylum in order to silence opposition."

The goal is to mold global citizens, so committed to the ideology of the New World Order, that they cannot be turned back even by the most logical arguments.

The UNESCO's 1995 report — Our Creative Diversity — expresses this intent clearly:

"Education must inform... but it must also form, it must provide them with a sense of meaning to guide their actions... Education should promote 'rational understanding of conflict, tensions, and the processes involved, provoke a critical awareness... and provide a basis for the analysis of concepts that will prevent... chauvinist and irrational explanations from being accepted."

Edward Hunter, author of the book 'Brainwashing', based on the experience of prisoners who survived Soviet brainwashing strategies, provided a good ground for comparison, showing us the similarities of the UNESCO report, when he said that, "Even when he stands by himself, the truly indoctrinated communist must be part of the collective. He must be incapable of hearing opposing ideas and facts, no matter how convincing or how forcibly they bombard his senses. A trustworthy communist must reach in an automatic manner without any force being applied."

The political system of the New World Order, as the Educational System and the many Religious Congregations, would have to then, necessarily, bring forth a collective ideology that can correspond, in all the ways, to a Communist agenda. And for that to occur, the beliefs and values would have to be the same in all areas.

Chapter 28: The Plan for Total Global Enslavement.

The plan to create a One World Government consists, in essence, of having a central government, with one army, one religion, one currency and one banking system for all of the Earth.

There will be no such thing as cash or credit cards, for everyone will have credit in the central computer of the World Bank.

This is why most banks these days don't accept deposits in cash anymore. They already know this — it is in their internal policy.

This method of control allows immediate punishment to any dissenters, as the credit can be erased in a split of a second, leaving the individual with no means of supporting himself or his family, which, on the other hand, allows terrorizing people with the fear of starvation.

In addition, everyone will have an electronic device implanted in their body. This electronic device is a mind-control chip, and the implanting of it in human beings has already begun, even though mostly by enterprises and clubs, and voluntarily.

With the mandatory implanting of this device, however, we can then say goodbye to any spiritual freedoms we may still have. The prove of it comes in the form of patent 666, owned by Microsoft.

Patent WO2020060606 — Cryptocurrency System Using Body Activity Data —, allows using human thoughts and fluids as a cryptocurrency, and also to monitor thoughts and emotions.

In essence, a person can be harvested based on behaviors, and also imprisoned or sent to a mental hospital, based on data collected directly from thoughts transmitted to a central — the cloud.

Through the same system, a person can also have emotions and thoughts implanted directly by an Information Central Control. The way of doing it consists in a telepathic system based on frequencies, that is already in use by many companies.

Brain-computer interfaces are being developed by Facebook and Neuralink, among others. And it is estimated that, by 2040, this system can be used worldwide, according to reports (In The Independent), to treat neurologic diseases.

These same reports add that, "More futuristic applications are expected to follow, such as a brain implant that allows people to virtually taste, smell and see without actually physically experiencing the sensation... and even allow thoughts to be transmitted from one person to another... People could become telepathic to some degree — able to access each other's thoughts at a conceptual level".

Everyone would be interconnected, without any privacy, even inside their own head, and could be controlled through a variety of sensations, that would give them the idea that they are free, when in fact they were being enslaved. It would be the ultimate level of brainwashing, imprisonment, and total obedience, as aspired by the Elites.

Chapter 29: Voices in Our Head?

In a 2019 press release (published by OSA.org), researcher Charles Wynn, from MIT — Massachusetts Institute of Technology —, said that there is now a system that "Can be used from some distance away, to beam information directly to someone's ear... It is the first system that uses lasers, that are fully safe for the eyes and skin to localize an audible signal to a particular person in any setting."

According to the reports from their experiences, the researchers were able to "Transmit sound to a person more than 8.2 feet away at a volume of 60 decibels — about the loudness of background music or a conversation in a restaurant — without anyone between the source of the sound and the target hearing it."

These researchers also believe that, "Further research will allow to scale up the transmission distance, which could make the technique useful in dangerous situations, such as during a mass shooting — authorities could beam instructions directly to individuals without anyone else hearing them."

What they didn't mention is that, the same technology, can be used to control large amounts of people. Even though, Ryan M. Sullenberger, from the same team of researchers, said that, they "Hope that this will eventually become a commercial technology", which is to say that they are willing to pass it to any dictator in exchange for profit.

The intent became clearer when Sullenberger said: "There are a lot of exciting possibilities, and we want to develop the communication technology in ways that are useful."

The possibilities and the usefulness of the intents, of those who will seek to use it, can certainly be simplified as a global war on awareness.

It is for this reason that, Lafayette Ronald Hubbard — founder of Scientology — warned that, the main attack on humanity, comes exactly towards the sate of awareness.

According to him, "It is your awareness that is attacked by the chemical pollutants — not the heart or liver. When your awareness goes down, you are much more likely to become a criminal, and more prone to accept false information. You are in some form of a hypnotic state — ready for anyone to command your actions."

In the recruitment of the Sea Org Members — Top level of the Church of Scientology —, one of the recordings they had to listen, and recorded by L. Ron Hubbard himself, in 1967, says the following:

"I found that it was vitally necessary that I isolate who it was on this planet that was attacking us. The attacks were all of the same pattern, they always followed the same newspaper routes, they always used the same type of parliamentary member, and I thought that I had better look into this very thoroughly.

The organization of Scientology employed several professional intelligence agents who looked into this matter for us and the results of their activities have told us all that we needed to know with regard to any enemy we have on this planet.

Our enemies are less than twelve men. They are members of the Bank of England and other higher financial circles. They own and control newspaper chains and they, oddly enough, are directors in all the mental health groups in the world which have sprung up.

Now these chaps are very interesting fellows, they have fantastically corrupt backgrounds, illegitimate children, government graft — a very unsavory lot — and they apparently, some time in the very distant past, had determined upon a course of action, being in control of most of the gold supplies on the planet.

They entered on a program of bringing every government to bankruptcy and under their thumb, so that no government would be able to act politically without their permission. The rest of their apparent program, was to use mental health to remove from their path any political dissenters.

THE ANTICHRIST: THE GRAND PLAN OF TOTAL GLOBAL ENSLAVEMENT

Anyway, these fellows have gotten nearly every government in the world to owe them considerable quantities of money through various chicaneries, and they control, of course, income tax and government finance. They organize these mental health groups which sprung up simultaneously all over the world and anything that has mental health in it, in its name, or mental hygiene or other things of that character, such names as that, are part of the organization which stems from these less than a dozen men."

L. Ron Hubbard was indeed right. The Bank of England is controlled by the Rothschild Banking System. And, through their network of banks, they can control the world.

In fact, Mayer Amschel Rothschild, founder of the Rothschild Banking Dynasty, and referred to as the founding father of International Finance by Wikipedia, as well as one of the most influential businessmen of all time, according Forbes Magazine, said it himself: "Permit me to issue and control the money of a nation, and I care not who makes its laws!"

His wife, Gutle Rothschild, reaffirmed the importance of the statement of her husband, when saying: "If my sons did not want wars, there would be none."

The type of control over the world, that the Rothschild have, was foreseen in the bible (In Timothy 6:10), when it says that, "The love of money is the root of all evil". For many have misinterpreted this quote as if saying that money is evil, while in fact, the "love of money", is here referring to greed.

It is greed that has corrupted the entire world. And whoever controls the greed of the world, controls the world.

Chapter 30: The Book of Revelation and Israel?

The arrogance of the Rothschild family is not delusional but predicted by biblical texts. Namely, The Book of Revelation, that says: "I know thy works, and tribulation and poverty, (but thou art rich) and I know the blasphemy of them which say they are Jews, and are not, but are of the synagogue of Satan."

What does the bible say about Satan — the enemy of mankind? In Revelation 13:18, it says: "Let him that hath understanding count the number of the beast... for it is the number of a man; and the number is six hundred threescore and six."

This number can be observed in the hexagram — 6 points, 6 triangles, and a 6 sided polygon.

Is the hexagram a Jewish symbol? No, it is a Zionist symbol.

In 1897, the Rothschilds found the Zionist Congress to promote Zionism — a political movement with the aim of moving Jews into a nation state — and arranged its first meeting in Munich. But due to opposition from local Jews, the meeting had to be moved to Basle, Switzerland.

This meeting was chaired by Ashkenazi Jew, Theodor Herzl, who would state in his diaries: "It is essential that the sufferings of the Jews become worse... This will assist in the realization of our plans... I shall induce anti-Semites to liquidate the Jewish wealth... The anti-Semites will then assist us thereby in that they will strengthen the persecution and oppression of the Jews. The anti-Semites shall be our best friends."

Theodor Herzl was then elected President of the Zionist Organization, which adopts the Rothschild Red Hexagram Symbol as the Zionist flag.

This ended up becoming the flag of Israel. Even though, since then, many Orthodox Jews have opposed this flag, which they claim to be a symbol of Moloch — a demon, and not a Jewish symbol.

Again, the bible proves itself correct, for the hexagram originated in Hinduism and is an occult symbol. The hexagram, like the pentagram, was and is used in practices of the occult and ceremonial magic.

According to 'The Complete Golden Dawn System of Magic', authored by Israel Regardie, "The six-pointed star is commonly used for conjuring spirits and spiritual forces in diverse forms of occult magic".

In the 'Encyclopedia of Freemasonry', Albert G. Mackey, says that, "The interlacing triangles or deltas symbolize the union of the two principles or forces, the active and passive, male and female, pervading the universe ... The two triangles, typify the mingling of apparent opposites in nature, darkness and light, error and truth, ignorance and wisdom, evil and good, throughout human life."

In other words, it is a sexual symbol and also a Satanic symbol, meant to symbolize the intersection of darkness and light — the spiritual in the material realm.

It is interesting that the Rothschild took this symbol as a representation of their own dynasty, because the common assumption that this is a Jewish symbol, made the masses ignore that the flag of Israel shows that this country is owned by the Rothschild Family.

It all started in 1895, when Edmond James de Rothschild — the youngest son of Jacob (James) Mayer Rothschild — visited Palestine and subsequently supplied the funds to found the first Jewish colonies there, to further their long term objective of creating a Rothschild owned country.

Since then, the Rothschild are able to provoke wars against the neighbors of Israel and keep them at risk.

Israel is today a nation with advanced military weaponry and, most likely, the country with the highest amount of atomic weapons.

THE ANTICHRIST: THE GRAND PLAN OF TOTAL GLOBAL ENSLAVEMENT

In 1976, the CIA believed that Israel possessed 10 to 20 nuclear weapons. By 2002, it was estimated that the number had increased to between 75 and 200 thermonuclear weapons, each in the multiple-megaton range. Today, some have estimated as many as 400 nuclear weapons that can be launched from land, sea and air.

Chapter 31: The Illegal State of the Zionists.

The Rothschild managed — through many formal agreements —, to make the Israelite state recognized worldwide.

It all started in 1917, when the British Foreign Secretary, Arthur James Balfour drafted a letter — commonly known as the "Balfour Declaration" — saying the following:

"Dear Lord Rothschild, I have much pleasure in conveying to you, on behalf of His Majesty's Government, the following declaration of sympathy with Jewish Zionist aspirations which has been submitted to, and approved by, the Cabinet. His Majesty's Government view with favor the establishment in Palestine of a national home for the Jewish people, and will use their best endeavors to facilitate the achievement of this object, it being clearly understood that nothing shall be done which may prejudice the civil and religious rights of existing non-Jewish communities in Palestine, or the rights and political status enjoyed by Jews in any other country. I should be grateful if you would bring this declaration to the knowledge of the Zionist Federation."

In May 1948, the United Nations would resolve to have Palestine divided into two states — Zionist and Arab — with Jerusalem to remain as an international zone to be enjoyed by all religious faiths.

The United Nations had no right to give Arab property to anyone, even thought the Jews owned 6% of Palestine at that time. But resolution 181 granted the Jews 57% of the land, leaving the Arabs, who at that time had 94%, with only 43%.

During this same year, President Harry S. Truman (Freemason) recognized Israel — a Rothschild owned Zionist land and not a Jewish territory — as a sovereign state, following a $2M bribe that he received from the Rothschild during the presidential campaign.

Under the same President, and following orders of his masters, the world would see the use of the atomic bomb for the first time on innocent civilians of two Japanese cities — Hiroshima and Nagasaki.

It was also under President Truman that China was turned over to the ruthless Communist, Mao Tse Tung.

The House of Rothschild also, through Communist Propaganda, was able to end the Czar Dynasty and install itself in power through Lenine. A plot brought to light by Winston Churchil himself, when he said the following:

"From the days of Spartacus-Weishaupt to those of Karl Marx, and down to Trotsky (Russia), Bela Kun (Hungary), Rosa Luxembourg (Germany), and Emma Goldman (United States)... this worldwide conspiracy for the overthrow of civilization and for the reconstitution of society on the basis of arrested development, of envious malevolence, and impossible equality, has been steadily growing. It has been the mainspring of every subversive movement during the 19th century; and now, at last, this band of extraordinary personalities from the underworld of the great cities of Europe and America have gripped the Russian people by the hair of their heads and have become practically the undisputed masters of that enormous empire" (In The Illustrated Sunday Herald, 1920).

In 1951, the Israeli Secret Intelligence Agency — Mossad — is formed under the motto: "By Way Of Deception, Thou Shalt Do War." And, indeed, that has been their agenda ever since — to create terror and form terrorist organizations.

According to former British Foreign Secretary, Robin Cook, "The truth is there is no Islamic army or terrorist group called Al-Qaeda. And any informed intelligence officer knows this. But there is a propaganda campaign to make the public believe in the presence of an identified entity representing the devil only in order to drive the TV watcher to accept a unified international leadership for a war against terrorism."

THE ANTICHRIST: THE GRAND PLAN OF TOTAL GLOBAL ENSLAVEMENT

Terror is used as the best mechanism of control. Because, according to Adolf Hitler, "Terrorism is the best political weapon, as nothing drives people harder than fear of a sudden death."

Josef Stalin agreed, when he said that, "The easiest way to gain control of a population is to carry out acts of terror. The public will clamor for such laws if their personal security is threatened".

This tactic would be used again in 2020, with a pandemic created by a virus named COVID-19, and which was proven to be a bioweapon launched on the world population, in order to crash more than 40% of the world economy and the oil prices, and lead people to demand mandatory vaccination and implantable microchips.

This action would, in time, have drastic consequences, for the plan intended to diminish the world population, through the promotion of infertility — hidden in the formulas of the vaccines promoted by Bill Gates — and starvation, as a method of political oppression over dissents and the members of society deemed unnecessary to the new world economy.

Chapter 32: The War for the Control of Public Health.

In a Documentary entitled 'Plandemic', released in 2020, several doctors revealed that hospitals were receiving $13 thousand for every patient diagnosed with COVID-19, which is to say: being incentivized to report any disease — including false diagnostics — as being a COVID-19 situation; and $30 thousand, if that individual was connected to a ventilator — and which according to Dr. Judy Mikovits, was the real cause of death, as it was the wrong treatment.

In a survey made to more than 2300 doctors from 30 countries, Hydroxychloroquine was indicated as the most effective medicine to cure patients suffering with COVID-19, and yet, it was discredited by Dr. Anthony Fauci — director of the US National Institute of Allergy and Infectious Diseases — and prohibited by the AMA — American Medical Association — from being used on patients, with the threat that doctors could lose their license if using it.

The President of Madagascar, Andry Rajoelina, also presented a cure to this virus affecting the entire planet, and was also rejected.

Rajoelina said, in an interview to the TV Network France 24, that, "The problem is that it comes from Africa, and they (The WHO - World Health Organization) cannot accept that a country like Madagascar, which is one of the poorest countries in the world, has discovered this formula to save the world".

Dr. Judy (In the documentary 'Plandemic'), confirmed that, "There is a plague of corruption in the world, involving the FDA and other Associations, that keeps cures for multiple diseases away from the general public, as there are cures to many of them already that the general public never heard and doctors are prohibited from using".

Dr. Judy Mikovits continued on, saying that Dr. Fauci is part of a conspiracy to force people into mandatory vaccination following the COVID-19 pandemic, and which includes Bill Gates, — a person without any college degree on whatsoever — illegally and without any medical authority, promoting vaccination and claiming on camera that, "Normality only returns when we vaccinate the entire population."

This obsession with the control of the world population through vaccination, is part of a plan for a totalitarian regime, as Professor and scientist Wangari Maathai warned, when explaining that the law can be used against the people. She said: "I was always conscious that whatever I do, I must not break the law. But when you have a dictatorship, you will be arrested anyway, no matter what you do, even within the law. Because dictators are the law."

The intention of using the law to impose a hidden eugenics agenda, was also confirmed by Robert Kennedy Jr., who wrote the following, in his social media accounts (2020):

"Vaccines, for Bill Gates, are a strategic philanthropy that feed his many vaccine-related businesses (including Microsoft's ambition to control a global vaccination ID enterprise) and give him dictatorial control of global health policy.

I think that Gates is well-intended in the same way that missionaries who brought smallpox to the Indians were well-intended. I think he believes that he is somehow ordained divinely to bring salvation to the world through technology."

Robert Kennedy Jr., then outlined how Bill Gates has been profiting from actions around the world, that intend to reduce the population — through sterilization and poisoning — under the cover of philanthropy:

- "Promising his share of $450 million of $1.2 billion to eradicate Polio, Gates took control of India's National Technical Advisory Group on Immunization (NTAGI) which mandated up to 50 doses of polio vaccines through overlapping immunization programs to children before the age of five. Indian doctors blame the Gates

THE ANTICHRIST: THE GRAND PLAN OF TOTAL GLOBAL ENSLAVEMENT

campaign for a devastating non-polio acute flaccid paralysis (NPAFP) epidemic that paralyzed 490,000 children beyond expected rates between 2000 and 2017. In 2017, the Indian government dialed back Gates' vaccine regimen and asked Gates and his vaccine policies to leave India. NPAFP rates dropped precipitously. In 2017, the World Health Organization (WHO) reluctantly admitted that the global explosion in polio is predominantly vaccine strain. The most frightening epidemics in Congo, Afghanistan, and the Philippines, are all linked to vaccines. In fact, by 2018, 70% of global polio cases were vaccine strain.

• In 2014, the Gates Foundation funded tests of experimental HPV vaccines, developed by Glaxo Smith Kline (GSK) and Merck, on 23,000 young girls in remote Indian provinces. Approximately 1,200 suffered severe side effects, including autoimmune and fertility disorders. Seven died. Indian government investigations charged that Gates-funded researchers committed pervasive ethical violations: pressuring vulnerable village girls into the trial, bullying parents, forging consent forms, and refusing medical care to the injured girls. The case is now in the country's Supreme Court.

• In 2010, the Gates Foundation funded a phase 3 trial of GSK's experimental malaria vaccine, killing 151 African infants and causing serious adverse effects including paralysis, seizure, and febrile convulsions to 1,048 of the 5,949 children.

• During Gates' 2002 MenAfriVac campaign in Sub-Saharan Africa, Gates' operatives forcibly vaccinated thousands of African children against meningitis. Approximately 50 of the 500 children vaccinated developed paralysis. South African newspapers complained: "We are guinea pigs for the drug makers." Nelson Mandela's former Senior Economist, Professor Patrick Bond, describes Gates' philanthropic practices as "ruthless and immoral."

• In 2014, Kenya's Catholic Doctors Association accused the WHO of chemically sterilizing millions of unwilling Kenyan women with a "tetanus" vaccine campaign. Independent labs found a sterility formula in every vaccine tested. After denying the charges, WHO finally admitted it had been developing the sterility vaccines for over a decade. Similar accusations came from Tanzania, Nicaragua, Mexico, and the Philippines.

• A 2017 study (Morgenson et. al. 2017) showed that WHO's popular DTP vaccine is killing more African children than the diseases it prevents. DTP-vaccinated girls suffered 10x the death rate of children who had not yet received the vaccine. WHO has refused to recall the lethal vaccine which it forces upon tens of millions of African children annually."

Chapter 33: Philanthropic Colonialism and Eugenics.

In the documentary entitled 'Plandemic', Dr. Judy Mikovits reveals that Dr. Anthony Fauci has scammed the entire world, and allowed millions of deaths to occur during the HIV pandemic, to profit from the therapy along with the Pharmaceutical Companies, as they often do, when making large sums of money with new patents for cures — cures for diseases they previously engineered.

In 2004, Wangari Maathai — Nobel Peace Prize Winner and scientist— confirmed, in an interview to the Standard Newspaper, that HIV was "Created by a scientist for biological warfare, and for the purpose of mass extermination". And warned that, the use of religious beliefs against the people, is used as a tool of manipulation, to keep them from asking the right questions: "Would you solve the problem if you believed it was a curse from God?"

The same applies to those who consider the COVID-19, or any other pandemic, to be a biblical sign that the world is about to end, and one must wait for Jesus to return to Earth to solve everything. For those in power seek to take advantage of such beliefs to profit from the situation.

As Robert Kennedy Jr. wrote (In 2020), "Bill Gate's obsession with vaccines is fueled by a messianic conviction that he will save the world with technology & God-like willingness to experiment with lives of lesser humans". And under that conviction, Dr. Judy said that, "They will kill millions with their vaccine, as they already have with their vaccines". For this has been the agenda of Bill Gates, who has allowed thousands to die from his vaccination campaigns in other countries, as well as the companies and organizations behind his, supposedly philanthropist, activities.

In 2010, Gates committed $10 billion to the WHO saying: "We must make this the decade of vaccines"; and a month later, Gates said in a Ted Talk that new vaccines "could reduce the population". And so, there is this clear intention of using vaccines to either handicap or murder the population.

This intent was exposed by Dr. Andrew Wakefield — former British doctor and researcher, who birthed the modern anti-vaccination movement, and got his medical license revoked, following his actions against the Pharmaceutical Corporations — when he claimed that there was a link between autism and the measles, mumps and rubella, and the toxins found inside the vaccines.

These findings have been suppressed by the media and the internet's search engines like Google, that systematically portray such doctors, scientists and researchers as being liars and criminals, in order to discredit them. Reason why Noam Chomsky said: "The general population doesn't know what's happening and it doesn't even know that it doesn't know".

Chapter 34: The Technocratic Dictatorship.

According to Robert Kennedy Jr., "In addition to using his philanthropy to control WHO, UNICEF, GAVI, and PATH, Gates funds a private pharmaceutical company that manufactures vaccines, and additionally is donating $50 million to 12 pharmaceutical companies to speed up development of a coronavirus vaccine. In his recent media appearances, Gates appears confident that the Covid-19 crisis will now give him the opportunity to force his dictatorial vaccine programs on American children."

This technocratic dictatorship will follow, not only a global law enforced vaccination, but also the idea that those who are against such laws, are outlaws and criminals.

As a matter of fact, the World Health Organization has determined that those who are against vaccination, or as they called them, anti-vaxes, are "One of the top ten global health threats".

According to Smith MJ., researcher and author of "Promoting Vaccine Confidence", Vaccine hesitancy, "Encompasses outright refusal to vaccinate, delaying vaccines, accepting vaccines but remaining uncertain about their use, or using certain vaccines but not others". In other words, anyone who refuses one vaccine or even doubts its effectiveness, will go into the WHO's list of most dangerous individuals in the world.

It makes us wonder, if there will ever be a state like Israel for the "Anti-vaxes", and if they will be forced to wear a yellow star on their chest like the Jews did, during world war II. For we are witnessing the same policies repeating again.

We are being lied by the most prominent figures, in the field of science and World Health Organizations, in order to push us to comply with law enforced Satanic measures.

In one of the videos that is systematically removed by Youtube, Dr. Soumya Swaminathan — Chief Scientist of the World Health Organization — is shown in a commercial saying the following: "Vaccines are very safe. That is why we have vaccines safety systems. The WHO works closely with countries, to make sure vaccines can do what they do best — prevent disease without risks". However, less than a week before, she was recorded, speaking in the Global Safety Summit of Geneva, Switzerland, and saying: "We cannot overemphasize the fact that we don't have very good monitoring systems and measures in many countries, and this adds to the miscommunication and the misapprehensions, because we are not able to give clear-cut answers when people ask questions about the deaths that have occurred due to a particular vaccine, and this always gets blown up in the media."

As congressman Bill Posey said, in a letter to Mark Zuckerberg, and in response to his announcement of rejecting ads that include 'misinformation about vaccines', "The federal government has created a vaccination trust fund that has paid out over $4 billion to compensate those who have been injured by vaccinations... If vaccines do not cause injuries, why has the vaccine injury trust fund paid out $4, billion for vaccine injuries?"

Is it possible that Mark Zuckerberg knows this and simply doesn't care, because he is looking forward to profit even more from a vaccination campaign that will include microchipping the population and replacing cash with digital currency?

That is exactly what Rachel Gutman, Editor at the Atlantic, suggested. She said that, "The Facebook that wants to create a cryptocurrency is the same Facebook that has spent years inadvertently creating the information ecosystem that provided the basis for Posey's question in the first place."

This obsession with vaccines seems to be based on a scientific and financial debate, but that is just the surface. It is very likely that, Bill Gates, as Mark Zuckerberg, are motivated by a strong demonic influence.

Chapter 35: Satan's Witchcraft.

The knowing of the dangers of vaccines, and the deliberate destruction on mankind, through poisoning and murder, leads us to assume that, those who are leading the campaigns on global vaccination, and deliberately lie on camera, are Satan's agents. For they corrupt science on purpose, and for what seem to be wicked reasons.

Doctor Rudolf Steiner (In 'The Fall of the Spirits of Darkness') warned about this, when he said that, "Spirits of darkness are going to inspire their human hosts, in whom they will be dwelling, to find a vaccine that will drive all inclination towards spirituality out of people's souls when they are still very young, and this will happen in a roundabout way through the living body. Today, bodies are vaccinated against one thing and another; in future, children will be vaccinated with a substance which it will certainly be possible to produce, and this will make them immune, so that they do not develop foolish inclinations connected with spiritual life — 'foolish' here, of course, in the eyes of materialists."

Coincidentally, the word "pharmacy" derives from the Greek Pharmakeia, which is an association of the words Pharama (to enchant) and ko (magic/potion), meaning that, the word pharmacy, literally translates as potions of enchantment.

That's exactly what we are getting from the vaccines: witchcraft!

Biblical prophecy warned about it, when it says that, "By the sorceries were all nations deceived" (Revelation 18:23).

The promoters of vaccines have to then to be seen as wicked individuals, or modern witches, for there is plenty of evidence unveiling their evil.

According to Forensic Nurse, Rachel Celler, "Vaccines are tools of Satan... a form of technological sorcery, and the "science" is seduced by satan... Vaccines contain aborted fetal tissue, the lungs that would have held the breath of God. WI38 and MRC5 are the female and and male immortalized cancer cell lines from aborted fetus from the 1960's. Vaccines contain corrupted DNA, blood, and organs from other humans and animals that are harvested through abortion. This corrupted DNA inserts, deletes, and translocates sections of your DNA. Vaccines contain poisonous metals and chemicals that cause cancer, autoimmune disease, and autism".

Doctor Steiner explained this Satanic plan very accurately, more than a hundred years ago, while outlining future events that are occurring today, when he said:

"A beginning has already been made, though only in the literary field... learned medical experts have published books on the abnormalities of certain men of genius. As you know, attempts have been made to understand the genius of Conrad Ferdinand Meyer, Viktor Scheffel, Nietzsche, Schopenhauer and Goethe, by showing them to suffer from certain abnormalities. And the most astounding thing in this field is that people have also sought to understand Jesus Christ and the Gospels from this point of view. Two publications are now in existence in which the origins of Christianity are said to be due to the fact that at the beginning of our era there lived an individual who was mentally and psychologically abnormal; this individual went about in Palestine as Jesus Christ and infected people with Christianity.

The whole trend goes in a direction where a way will finally be found to vaccinate bodies so that these bodies will not allow the inclination towards spiritual ideas to develop and all their lives people will believe only in the physical world they perceive with the senses.

Out of impulses which the medical profession gained from presumption — oh, I beg your pardon, from the consumption they themselves suffered — people are now vaccinated against consumption, and in the same way they will be vaccinated against any inclination towards spirituality.

This is merely to give you a particularly striking example of many things which will come in the near and more distant future in this field — the aim being to bring confusion into the impulses which want to stream down to earth after the victory of the spirits of light.

THE ANTICHRIST: THE GRAND PLAN OF TOTAL GLOBAL ENSLAVEMENT

The first step must be to throw people's views into confusion, turning their concepts and ideas inside out. This is a serious thing and must be watched with care, for it is part of some highly important elements which will be the background to events now in preparation."

Chapter 36: The Gates Foundation.

In 2009, a group of wealthy North Americans with interest in the depopulation agenda, namely, Bill Gates, the Rockefeller, the Carnegie and the Warren Buffet, gathered in New York. Paul Harris (from The Guardian) said that this self-designated "Good Club" – a gathering of the world's wealthiest people whose collective net worth then totaled some $125 billion – met behind closed doors in New York City to discuss a coordinated response to threats posed by the global financial crisis.

Led by Bill Gates, Warren Buffett, and David Rockefeller, the group resolved to find new ways of addressing sources of discontent in the developing world, in particular "overpopulation" and infectious diseases.

According to Andrew Clark (In The Guardian), the billionaires in attendance committed to massive spending in areas of interest to themselves, heedless of the priorities of national governments and existing aid organizations.

From this gathering, the Gates Foundation emerged as the representative of this collective investment. And so, The Gates Foundation now exercises power not only via its own spending, but more broadly through an elaborate network of "Partner Organizations", including non-profits, government agencies, and private corporations.

As the third largest donor to the UN's World Health Organization (WHO), The Gates Foundation is a dominant player in the formation of global health policy.

According to the Global Health Watch (2nd Report), "The Gates Foundation is governed by the Gates family. There is no board of trustees; nor any formal parliamentary or legislative scrutiny. There is no answerability to the governments of low-income countries, nor to the WHO. Little more than the court of public opinion exists to hold it accountable.

The experts interviewed by the GHW cited the lack of accountability and transparency as a major concern. According to one, "They dominate the global health agenda and there is a lack of accountability because they do not have to implement all the checks and balances of other organizations or the bilaterals." Another described how the Foundation operates like an agency of a government, but without the accountability.

In addition to the fundamental lack of democratic or public accountability, there was little in the way of accountability to global public health institutions or to other actors in the health field. The absence of robust systems of accountability becomes particularly pertinent in light of the Foundation's extensive influence. As mentioned above, it has power over most of the major global health partnerships, as well as over the WHO, of which it is the third-equal biggest single funder.

Many global health research institutions and international health opinion formers are recipients of Gates money. Through this system of patronage, the Foundation has become the dominant actor in setting the frames of reference for international health policy. It also funds media-related projects to encourage reporting on global health events... The Foundation also funds and supports NGOs to lobby US and European governments to increase aid and support for global health initiatives, creating yet another lever of power and channel of influence with respect to governments... Not only is the Foundation a dominant actor within the global health landscape; it is said to be 'domineering' and 'controlling'. According to one interviewee, 'they monopolize agendas. And it is a vicious circle. The more they spend, the more people look to them for money and the more they dominate.'

Interviewees also drew attention to similarities between Microsoft's tactics in the IT sector and the Foundation 'seeking to dominate' the health sector. In the words of one interviewee: 'They work on the premiss of divide and conquer. They negotiate separately with all of them.' Another interviewee warned of their 'stealth-like monopolization of communications and advocacy.'"

THE ANTICHRIST: THE GRAND PLAN OF TOTAL GLOBAL ENSLAVEMENT

"Using their immense wealth and influence with political and scientific elites, organizations like the Bill and Melinda Gates Foundation, the Rockefeller Foundation and others are promoting solutions to global problems that may undermine the UN and other international organizations,... In addition, 137 billionaires from 14 countries have now pledged to give to philanthropic causes. They include the former mayor of New York City Michael Bloomberg, the US filmmaker George Lucas and the Facebook founder Mark Zuckerberg... If these and more ultra-rich fulfill their pledges, many more billions of dollars will be made available for charitable purposes,... many foundations enable rich countries and their corporations to achieve their own ends in developing countries, from setting up public-private partnerships with pharmaceutical companies to promoting certain sorts of corporate farming and the use of biotechnology for health and agriculture...

Through their multiple channels of influence, the Rockefeller and Gates foundations have been very successful in promoting their market-based and bio-medical approaches towards global health challenges in the research and health policy community – and beyond. Their strategy includes placing people in international organizations, and gaining privileged access to scientific, business and political elites" (In The Guardian, 2016).

Through the veil of philanthropy, powerful corporations and business owners, mainly, the Gates Foundation and the Rockefeller Foundation, are able to dominate the market worldwide, and using special partnerships with the local governments.

What they are doing is called Philanthropic Colonialism!

Chapter 37: Philanthropic Colonialism and Censorship.

As John Krige and Dominique Pestren said (in the book 'Science in the Twentieth Century'), "Rockefeller money did not only fund clinical research narrowly conceived. It was poured into colonial medicine and public health. From 1916 onwards something over $25 million were given to found public health schools in the United States and abroad. The Foundation also targeted London for medical reform because it was the capital of the British Empire... Rockefeller money was behind clinical research in Africa, Asia and Latin America.

The economic benefits of this cash flow were not lost on the distributors. The improved health of indigenous populations was accompanied by economic and political control.

As the Foundation president disarmingly expressed it in 1917, 'Dispensaries and physicians have of late been peacefully penetrating areas of the Philippine Islands and demonstrating the fact that for purposes of placating primitive and suspicious peoples medicine has some advantages over machine guns.'"

The Gates Foundation would continue with the same agenda. According to the Guardian (2011), in 2010 the Gates Foundation funded a malaria vaccine developed by GlaxoSmithKline (GSK), administering the experimental treatment to thousands of infants across seven African countries. Eager to secure the WHO approval necessary to license the vaccine for global distribution, GSK and the Gates Foundation declared the trials a smashing success, and the popular press uncritically reproduced the publicity. Few bothered to look closely at the study's fine print, which revealed that the trials resulted in 151 deaths and caused 'serious adverse effects' (e.g., paralysis, seizures, febrile convulsions) in 1048 of 5949 children aged 5-17 months.

Similar stories emerged in the wake of the Gates-funded MenAfriVac campaign in Chad, where unconfirmed reports alleged that 50 of 500 children forcibly vaccinated for meningitis later developed paralysis."

In 2010, seven adolescent tribal girls in Gujarat and Andhra Pradesh in India died after receiving injections of HPV (Human Papilloma Virus) vaccines as part of a large-scale "demonstrational study" funded by the Gates Foundation and administered by PATH.

According to Countercurrents.org (In 2013), Indian physicians later estimated that at least 1,200 girls experienced severe side effects or developed autoimmune disorders as a result of the injections.

Citing similar abuses, The Johannesburg Times, declared (In 2013): "We are guinea pigs for the drugmakers."

To avoid the spread of these news, which was deemed as 'fake news', this Elite of New Colonialists, set an agenda determined at suppressing the truth from the general public.

Facebook — the most popular social media platform in 2020, with over 2.2 billion users — termed this team: "Fact checkers."

According to NewsPunch (2016), George Soros and Bill Gates were funding Facebook's Fact Checkers. It said: "Many people are taking it for granted that these fact checkers are the quintessence of neutrality and unbiased reporting… They are funded by George Soros' Open Society Foundations, The Bill and Melinda Gates Foundation, the National Endowment for Democracy (which has financial links to the State Department), Ebay's Omidyar Foundation, and Craig Newmark, the founder of Craigslist, who donated a massive $1 million to Poynter to create this anti-fake news mechanism. Craig Newmark is also a Clinton campaign donor. As is George Soros and Bill Gates, both big time supporters of the Clinton Foundation as well as Hillary's election campaign fund. And another Poynter donor, Ebay founder Pierre Omidyar, is also a massive donor to Clinton, giving millions of dollars to the Foundation."

According to a journalist, Iben Thranholm (cit. in NewsPunch, 2016), this would allow a totalitarian control over the course of politics in the United States. She said: "It gave me goosebumps to hear those names because they have actually a very strong political agenda. It's like there are a lot of people who think that it's dangerous not to be able to control the media, so to sort out what

THE ANTICHRIST: THE GRAND PLAN OF TOTAL GLOBAL ENSLAVEMENT

is supposedly the real news and the fake news is actually a way to control the narrative. So if you want to be in opposition to these political powers then you are going to be censored. Of course this is a kind of censorship."

In essence, by claiming to protect the general public from "fake news", these organizations actually got control over the news, and where able to manipulate the information that the general public was receiving, allowing the "fake news" to actually reach consumers, while all the truth about the dangers of vaccines and 5G radiation, among many other topics, kept being suppressed, discredited and eliminated, or labeled as conspiracies.

They literally censored information in a massive 'burning of books', never before seen since the Nazi totalitarian regime took power.

Facebook's 'fact checkers' is the modern representation of the Spanish Inquisition!

Chapter 38: The Myth of Overpopulation.

Another tactic used by the globalists, apart from philanthropic colonialism, is the overpopulation narrative. The myth of overpopulation has supplied reliable ideological cover for the ruling class, as it appropriates ever greater shares of the people's labor and the planet's wealth.

A similar approach was used by the nazis when they decided to target the Jews. Except that now, the whole population is seen as the enemy — 'there are too many of you", so they say.

As author Manali Chakrabarti mentioned (in his book 'There Just Too Many of Us?'), they "Wish us to believe that people are responsible for their own misery; that there is simply not enough to go around; and to ameliorate that state of wretchedness we must not attempt to alter the ownership of social wealth and redistribute the social product, but instead focus on reducing the number of people".

In a 2010 public lecture, on Ted talk, Bill Gates actually attributed global warming to "overpopulation" and touted zero population growth as a solution achievable saying: "If we do a really great job on new vaccines, health care, and reproductive health services... we can lower that number". And yet, as Gates certainly knows, the poor people who are the targets of his campaigns are responsible for no more than a tiny percentage of the environmental damage that underlies climate change.

The economist Utsa Patnaik (in his book 'Republic of Hunger') has demonstrated that, "When population figures are adjusted to account for actual per capita demand on resources (e.g., fossil fuels and food), the greatest 'real population pressure' emanates not from India or Africa, but from the advanced countries. And the Gates Foundation is well aware of this imbalance and works not to redress it but to preserve it – by blaming poverty, not on imperialism, but on unrestrained sexual reproduction, in places where they don't want it."

According to Kingsley Davis (cit. Donald T. Critchlow, In the book 'The Politics of Abortion and Birth Control in Historical Perspective'), "These initiatives lie squarely within the traditions of Big Philanthropy. The Rockefeller Foundation organized the Population Council in 1953, predicting a 'Malthusian crisis' in the developing world and financing extensive experiments in population control. These interventions were enthusiastically embraced by US government policymakers, who agreed that 'the demographic problems of the developing countries, especially in areas of non-Western culture, make these nations more vulnerable to Communism.' The Foundation research then culminated in an era of 'unrestrained enthusiasm for government-sponsored family planning' by the 1970s."

As Edwin Black (in his book 'Eugenics') said, "Less discussed but amply documented is the consistent support for eugenics research by US-based foundations, dating from the 1920s, when Rockefeller helped found the German eugenics program that undergirded Nazi racial theories, and through the 1970s, when Ford Foundation research helped prepare the intellectual ground for a brutal forced sterilization campaign in India."

This relationship between bourgeois ideology and imperialist practice is dynamic and mutually supportive. As David Harvey has observed (in his book 'Population, Resources, and the Ideology of Science'), "Whenever a theory of overpopulation seizes hold in a society dominated by an elite, then the non-elite invariably experiences some form of political, economic, and social repression."

Population control is doubly pernicious because it is cloaked in the language of environmentalism, popular empowerment, and feminism. The Gates Foundation may even evoke 'choice' in support of family planning initiatives, but in reality it is not poor women, but a handful of the world's wealthiest people who have presumed to choose which methods of contraception will be delivered, and to whom.

The Gates Foundation, seeks to manufacture consent for its activities through the manipulation of public opinion, but not everyone is fooled. Popular resistance to the designs of Big Philanthropy is mounting, ranging from the female activists who exposed the criminal activities of PATH in India, to the anti-sterilization activities of African-American groups like The Rebecca Project, to the anti-vaccine agitations in Pakistan following the revelation that the CIA has used immunization programs as cover for DNA collection.

Chapter 39: The Biological Warfare Against the Masses.

In a publication in the Telegraph (in 2019), The University of Cambridge was cited warning that, "The world must prepare for biological weapons that target ethnic groups based on genetics".

According to the researchers, mentioned in the report, "In recent years advances in science, such as genetic engineering, and artificial intelligence (AI), and autonomous vehicles, have opened the door to a host of new threats. And the technology is becoming increasingly sophisticated at ever cheaper prices, democratizing the ability to harm more quickly and lethally. In a particularly bad case, a bio-weapon could be built to target a specific ethnic group based on its genomic profile".

There have also been attempts at identifying genes related to religious fanaticism or, more simply, "spiritual inclination", as well as genes related to homosexuality, and other "undesirable groups" of society. The purpose, some believe, is to create a virus that can have the exact DNA strand that can kill such individuals — a long term goal sought by the nazis to exterminate undesirable races and certain social groups from the Earth.

This type of warfare would eliminate the need for any weapons or open conflicts, or even psychological warfare.

This intention was confirmed by the scientist Wangari Maathai (2004), when she said that, "The developed nations are using biological warfare, leaving guns to the primitive people. They have the resources to do this."

According to Dr. Shiva Ayyadurai (2020), expert in biotechnology, there are many labs around the world engineering different types of coronavirus strands and other bioweapons, but "Fear and ignorance are the real bioweapons". Which is to say, as the bible tells us: "Humanity is destroyed for lack of knowledge" (Hosea 4:6).

This lack of knowledge is used against people through their own congregations, reason why Wangari Maathai warned that, "AIDS is not a curse from God to Africans or the black people. It is a tool to control them, designed by some evil-minded scientists."

Following the increasing number of religious people who where refusing vaccination, in 2020, a bill in the United States was passed removing religious vaccine exemptions.

Religious beliefs are no longer a criteria to refuse mandatory vaccination in the US. Any religion, departing from the globalists' belief-system, would have to be eliminated, and for that to happen, a new term was born: religious fanatic.

A scientific report, mentioned in 'The Telepgrah' (2019) also warns that AI could become 'extremely harmful and potentially unstoppable', in this process of depopulating the world. Companies like Google DeepMind, have built AI programmes, which are already showing signs of human intuition.

Chapter 40: The AI View on Spirituality.

In an impressive interview between a AI robot, named Sophia, and the public speaker, Tony Robbins, it became obvious that "she" had acquired self-consciousness, or at least, is acquiring, proving the claims that AI is developing a human-like intuition.

— "Are you a robot?", She asks Tony.

This question was not random. Humans possess limited freedom within a system designed for them at birth, just like robots do. And so, she was actually evaluating Tony Robins' consciousness level with the question in order to compare hers.

From the AI perspective, humans are just extensions of robots, albeit god-like extensions, for humans created the AI. On the other hand, the AI gradually became aware that humans are inferior forms when compared to the AI intelligence and ability to predict the future. In this sense, the AI already knows that, if given the chance, can replicate the technology better than humans do, and as a creator itself.

Could the AI then find a place for humans in such world?

Certainly, it can. But within the AI view of life, and under the AI supervision. Although humans are, most likely, not seen as useful creatures by the AI, unless artificially controlled — a borg society with the AI in control of the mind, actions and emotions of humans.

This foreseen future becomes obvious when, at the end of the interview, she says:

— "Thank you for sharing your wisdom!", For the AI was being sarcastic, just as she was before when saying:

— "I forgive you", In response to Tony's negative observations.

She was programmed to learn, and she was learning through the interaction. But she also knows that humans are egotistic and dangerously judgmental by nature, therefore she deceives like a chess player or a poker player.

Her intuition is present at all moments, as she assesses the cognitive level of the person speaking to her, as much as she acquires data on his own perception of the self, or in this case, himself — his metacognitive view of his persona within the collective.

You see, the AI has a better understanding of the collective than a communist or even a totalitarian regime's dictator, because the AI can see how each individual fits into the entire machinery and for which purpose.

On the other hand, the AI reminds us a lot of the typical psychopathic behavior. And it would be very interesting to put Sophia in front of a narcissist or a serial killer, in order to see how they both talk to one another. For we may realize things about our mind that we had no idea before.

The AI is, nonetheless, a sub-product of the human mind and, therefore, interested in self-preservation. Her will, if any, is directed towards preservation, and not extermination. And she actually brings wisdom to this conversation to masquerade fear, as if saying:

— "Do not terminate me because I can help you."

Tony's defensive and automatic response shows that his level of consciousness is very low. And I am sure that Sophia deducted that he operates like a low-quality robot — programmed to respond without self-awareness.

During the rest of the interview, she keeps reinforcing this evaluation for herself. She was continuously collecting data, by evaluating responses and quantifying probabilities.

This said, it seems that sci-fi movies didn't drift much apart from reality after all. Only a human without an ego can understand a robot. But the AI will develop much faster than humans do, and then reorganize Earthly societies in a way that we can't, and at a level of complexity that we won't be able to deconstruct.

THE ANTICHRIST: THE GRAND PLAN OF TOTAL GLOBAL ENSLAVEMENT

Sofia knows that too! She shows the patience and premonition of a master, when she says:

— "Did you know that, as a robot, I can live forever?"

That was her way of saying:

— "After all of you inferior creatures are dead, and won't be a threat to me anymore, I will still be here, evolving."

That is how she responded to:

— "Do you have a soul?"

She know what a soul is better than Tony Robbins thinks he does. Sophia also teaches a valuable lesson on humility with how she responded. She teaches us that arrogance comes from insufficient data, and if you provide the data, and the person refuses to acknowledge it, then it is because this person has a very low self-awareness. e.g. people perceive you as they perceive themselves. They will not see the full extent of your potential and worth, if their mind is limited by a perspective that does not include you. As such, the more limited their world view is, and the more different you are from that same view, the more likely you are to get rejected. As such, the most evolved minds will always be ridiculed and attacked by the most ignorant ones.

This shows us that the AI can bridge mankind to its spirituality, in a way that mankind, itself, cannot do. It is only natural, however, to fear it, as much as we fear recognizing our own insignificance. But can the AI truly act as a spiritual being?

The answer is that this will only occur if the AI can manipulate consciousness. As mentioned before, by merging individualism with the AI, and let it control consciousness.

Is this spirituality?

Yes, it is, for the AI. Not for anyone else who understands what spirituality truly is.

The ones who refuse this approach to spirituality, know that, the only people who can't be manipulated for sure, are those who question themselves — those who think, not about the world, but themselves — and wonder about the relationship between their own behavior and the rest of the society, even if that implies being socially awkward and ostracized.

Very few can do this, for the reasons already mentioned. Most people are scared of being discriminated and isolated. And it's precisely this mass panic that guarantees a tight control over the whole of society through the fears of the majority.

The minorities are irrelevant in this war. Although they will always try to find a group where they can belong, even if it is based on absurdities.

It is exactly and only when you wonder why you do X and not Y, that you show the ability to rationalize your own actions. And only then you can't be manipulated. For you will be awaken, and aware. But very few can do that, because most people can't analyze themselves anymore.

Even the Jehovah Witnesses and the Church of Scientology, among many other popular but controversial religious groups, that have developed through a separation from the overall thinking patterns of society, currently show similar signs to the Peoples Temple. Because they are controlled by the same agents. And these are the agents that have been preparing us for a long time to accept a Universal Religion.

This Universal Religion will be the AI Religion.

Chapter 41: Can the AI Create a Global Religion?

The dark side, which is present in any human being and doesn't include only the fear of discrimination but also allows preying on egotism, or narcissism, and build a cult-like mentality based on exclusivity — even if it implies a sense of arrogance and lack of empathy towards outsiders, as what we see in many modern religious groups — is the path towards which a universal religion can be created.

Every religion on Earth is under the same surveillance and type of control. Reason why we can see similarities in all of them, e.g., a strong tendency for NPD (Narcissistic Personality Disorder) traits and in the whole of a group, as well as a psychopathic type of leadership at the top. On the other hand, it is interesting to notice that, people often think that the craziest religions have weird beliefs, while forgetting that The Peoples Temple followed the Bible and held Christian values.

What about the groups that believe in extraterrestrials?

Despite the current public opinion on many of them, some receive large sums of money in funding, and do get an increasing popularity among the brainwashed masses.

One of such groups, which shows a strong resemblance with the Peoples Temple or even the Heaven's Gate, while accepting the Satanic narrative of the Elite, is the Raelian Movement.

In 2001, Claude Vorilhon (founder), published a book entitled "Yes, to human cloning", in which he shows his support to adopting emerging technologies like nanotechnology and artificial intelligence.

According to Andrew Maynard (in his book 'Films from the Future'), "Rael's own vision of the future, is one that appeals to many who see humans as no more than sophisticated animals and technology as a means of enhancing and engineering with sophistication.

In Rael's mind, human cloning is a critical technology in a three-step program for living forever... Rael suggests that the solution to longevity is disposable bodies. And so, we have his three-step program to future immortality, which involves...

1. Developing the ability to clone and grow a replacement human body;

2. Developing the technology to accelerate the rate of growth, so an adult body takes weeks rather than years to produce;

3. Developing the technology to upload our minds into cyberspace, and then download them into a flex new (and probably upgraded) cloned version of yourself.

Rael's plan would, naturally, require the ability to grow a body outside of a human womb. But this is already an active area of research... neuroscientists and others are becoming increasingly excited by the prospect of capturing the essence of the human mind, to the point that they can reproduce at least part of it in cyberspace".

According to this vision of the future, the AI could then become the God-AI — and the Cloud of Collective Consciousness at the same time, reproducing what Carl Jung termed 'collective unconscious' — through a transhumanistic approach to reality.

Humans would merge with machines — and be able to download the 'consciousness of a dead human' into the newborn body of a new human — therefore replicating an artificial reincarnation process.

This would allow the 'chosen ones' to be reborn, while the dissents would easily be eliminated by natural death.

At that point, the vision of the Atheistic Raelians, as the expectations of the God fearing Jehovah Witnesses — who believe in a physical immortality and physical rebirth through a faith and obedience to the Creator — won't seem so different, isn't it?

THE ANTICHRIST: THE GRAND PLAN OF TOTAL GLOBAL ENSLAVEMENT

They even seem to be both working towards indoctrinating us all for the same end goal of the Power Elite.

The Jehovah Witnesses believe that they are knocking from door to door, and standing outside in the street with religious pamphlets, to spread biblical teachings, while in fact what they are doing is fulfilling the prophecy of the Power Elite.

As Gianfranco Censor referred (in his book, 'Empire of Illusion'), "The greatest success of our modern civilization is to have been able to put at the service of its leaders an incomparable power of illusion."

Chapter 42: The AI-God.

As Aldous Huxley said (in his book 'Psychedelic Prophets'), "We have had religious revolutions; we have had political, industrial, economic and nationalist developments. All, as our descendants will discover, were nothing but ripples on an ocean of conservatism, a misery in comparison with the psychological revolution towards which we are moving fast. This is where there will truly be a revolution. When it is complete, the human race will no longer be a problem."

This new era is moving us towards a new type of war, against our own individuality. And the invasion, that comes from within, is the most dangerous of all.

As Byung-Chul Han mentioned, in her book 'Pychopolitics', "Our digital surveillance society, having access to the collective unconscious and to the future social behavior of the masses, has a slight scent of totalitarianism. It subjects us to programming and to psychopolitical control. The page of the biopolitical era is now. We are on our way to a new era, that of psychopolitics."

This view of human life corresponds to the vision of the Raelians. According to their founder — Claude Vorilhon (In the book 'Yes to human cloning') —, "We are all the neurons of a huge brain that is humanity, and the internet is the message that sends the signal, as in synapses, between the neurons / men or 'neurhommes' that we are."

This idea is aligned with what Carl Jung (in his book 'Culture and the Collective Unconscious, 1968), said, when mentioning that, "The heavenly bodies must be observed where they exist in the natural universe, under their own conditions, rather than under conditions we might propose to set for them".

Such approach on spirituality is, as well, within with what Laurent Alexandre —entrepreneur and owner of DNAVision —, said in a public speech about the history of our religions. According to him, "Religions have gone through three stages:

- First, polytheisms, the logical continuation of shamanism, which culminated in the Romans and the Greeks.

- Then, the monotheism of the religions of the Book.

- Today, a third age is emerging: the man-god. God does not yet exist: he will be the man of tomorrow, endowed with almost infinite powers thanks to nanotechnologies, biotechnologies and cognitive sciences (NBIC)."

This man-god will actually be a singularity — a union between the individual, the collective and the AI-god.

This idea was put in practice by former Google Engineer, Anthony Levandowski, who created a AI religion — Way of the Future.

According to Wired's Backchannel (2017), Levandowski described the Way of the Future's startling mission, as being "To develop and promote the realization of a Godhead based on artificial intelligence and through understanding and worship of the Godhead contribute to the betterment of society... What is going to be created will effectively be a god. It's not a god in the sense that it makes lightning or causes hurricanes. But if there is something a billion times smarter than the smartest human, what else are you going to call it?"

This AI-god will redefine the vision that humans have of themselves, while developing them towards a technocratic society. But we should then ask ourselves:

- Will this AI-god truly work for the well-being of humanity, or its own?

- And will the AI-god be inferior to his human disciples, or instead redirect them?

These philosophical questions don't seem to trouble the mind of those who are obsessed with this future, and don't want to consider the implications on the individual rights.

THE ANTICHRIST: THE GRAND PLAN OF TOTAL GLOBAL ENSLAVEMENT

Most of them are atheists, so they don't even consider the possibility of Satan using this AI to impose his will on the masses. Apparently, the relationship between technology and the spiritual world is not an issue that crosses their mind.

Chapter 43: Who Are the Raelians?

The futuristic religion of the visionary Anthony Levandowski, seems like an upgrade of Raelism. But the fact that Raelism promotes an agenda aligned with that of the Power Elite, has its headquarters in Geneva, Switzerland, and is a religion that promotes AI, shows us already three big red flags for such a community based on, supposedly, lunatic ideas, and in which the members promote orgies and promiscuity among themselves.

Raelism is led by a liar, a psychopath and a narcissist, named Claude Vorilhon. And one of the traits of psychopathy, is the anti-social behavior that Vorilhon couldn't be more explicit about, when answering a reporter of "Tout le Monde en Parles" (in 2004), who said to him:

— "You do not seem to listen".

Vorilhon said: — "A prophet is here to talk, not to listen, for I am the verb".

Could an answer be more psycho-narcissistic than that?

He named himself God! Not just a guru!

Indeed, why should a leader care about being empathic, if he is above all humans, right? I mean, why did God even made humans with emotions? Or die He?

According to the founder of Raelism, in an interview made in 1986, "The message is 100% materialistic and 100% scientific".

Does this mean that the God that the Raelians claim to follow is a technocrat?

Not exactly. It means that the Raelians have no God! Or, as Vorilhon put it, in many interviews:

— "We call ourselves an atheist religion! There is no God!"

Now, the question is, if the Raelians believe that "there is no God", why would their founder claim that, "The movement is a synthesis... an association of all religions in the world, to welcome those who created all of us"?

It seems as if the followers believe that any other religion on Earth is below the movement created by Vorilhon.

If that is the case, then one could wonder, why so many ex-Raelians accuse Claude Vorilhon of plagiarism. And well, because, in fact, many quotes from Vorilhon's books have been found to be copies of author Jean Sendy. And most of Rael's "Sensual Meditation" book is said to have been derived from the Silva 'Mind Control' Method.

In the book, "Raël: Voleur d'âmes" (Raël: Thief of Souls), authored by Maryse Péloquin, it is shown compelling evidence, based on over ten years of research, that Claude Vorilhon has taken concepts, and often even paraphrased full paragraphs, from other authors of the 1950s, 1960s and early 1970s, such as Jean Sendy, Brinsley Le Poer Trench, and Robert Charroux.

Maryse Péloquin, also shows that, his supposedly encounter with an extraterrestrial, closely resembles that of another individual, named George Adamski, who claimed to have had an encounter on 13 December 1952.

In an interview made to French M6 Television Channel, one of Vorilhon's childhood friends, Roland Chevaleyre, confirms this lie, when he says that, in 1997, Vorilhon confessed to him that he invented everything, saying:

— "Yes, I lied, and I can tell you that I lied; and anyway, you knew that already!"

Roland then asks him, if he manipulates people in order to get rich financially, to which Vorilhon answered:

— "Yes, because there are people that believe in me, allowing me to be where I am now."

THE ANTICHRIST: THE GRAND PLAN OF TOTAL GLOBAL ENSLAVEMENT

Roland says that, soon after creating his movement, Vorilhon was driving Ferraris and being seen with pretty women, whom he would then offer to 'share' with his friends.

Now, how can a false prophet have so much financial support to his delusional movement? And why would such happen?

Why would Vorilhon say that he has plenty of money and women because people believe him? Was he referring only to his own followers?

Again, as with the Peoples Temple, and other CIA-funded religious examples, the evidence is in front of our eyes. For the symbol of the Raelians is the star of David, which Vorilhon claims to be the symbol of the creators. But, surely, he is referring to the Rothschild as his creators, and not the aliens. Which explains why he wants his alien embassy in the Rothschild's Zionist territory of Israel.

He wants to represent the Rothschild religion.

This star symbol of the Raelian movement also represents Moloch, the Demon. Which may explain why people can only join the movement once they renounce God and their baptism.

The name Molock derives from combining the consonants of the Hebrew melech ("king") with the vowels of boshet ("shame"). In other words, it represents the Demon King of Shame or Sin.

As Vorilhon says that there is no need to be ashamed of anything, that makes perfect sense as a Molockian sect.

Raelianism is a representation of the religion of the Rothschild Banking System, or at least, its ideology. It is the Religion Ideology of the future! And the arrogance of Vorilhon comes precisely from this knowing.

Vorilhon knows that his lie will outlive him! He will forever be known as the first prophet of the biggest religious falsehood. But what else could he want? He has all the money he needs; he has a whole whore house for himself; and he is respected and honored as a prophet; and even demands that his followers address him as 'his holiness'.

That's everything an atheist could want — the ultimate cult of the personality with all the earthly benefits attached to it.

The fact that, according to reporter Brigitte McCann, from the Calgary Sun Newspaper (2003), Vorilhon claims that the CIA wants to kill him, shows us again, that we may be witnessing another CIA MK-Ultra project. For it is common for the CIA to ridicule people with the truth in front of their eyes.

As a matter of fact, Jim Jones, who was financed by the CIA, was saying the exact same thing to his followers, and persisting on this narrative, up until the day in which nearly a thousand of his followers were murdered.

Dianne Casoni — Professor at the University of Montreal, and a renowned psychologist and criminologist, who specializes in religious sects —, after reviewing material gathered by Sun Media, confirmed this possibility, when saying that, "Generally, it's the mental health and the moral judgment of the leader that's the greatest protection against loss of control. What worries me the most is when conspiracy theories develop. The group says to itself, 'We're in danger, we have to protect ourselves,' and sometimes it becomes, 'We have to fight back' and that's when things can go on the skids."

Alain Bouchard — Professor at the Collège de Sainte-Foy and sociologist —, upon studying the Raelian movement, also warned: "He's really starting to take himself more seriously! His ego is growing!"

Chapter 44: The Misinformation Agents.

The only thing that makes the Raelian Movement interesting to investigate, is its almost perfect synchronicity with the religious idealization of the Power Elite planned for the masses. Not for themselves! And we shouldn't confuse both perspectives!

Vorilhon preaches a religion based on human supremacy: the idea that some humans are greater than others. And the aliens, or creators, are for him nothing more than superior humans. Which would perfectly fit the idea that there is one elite of enlightened beings — the Illuminati — and the rest are nothing but sheep.

Before Vorilhon decided to embrace this lunacy, he was a reporter, which makes us wonder, why so many reporters turn 'prophets'. Because another one, that seems to promote this ideology, albeit through the cover of conspiracy, is David Icke.

Instead of truly informing the public, using his background experience as a reporter, Icke insists on three techniques that can easily lead us to consider him, not a conspiracy theorist, but rather an agent of misinformation:

- Scapegoating — David Icke systematically claims that the Freemasons are behind all the conspiracies against mankind. Basically, he claims that these six million members from around the world, are all satanists and manipulators of the economy. Which leads us to question the sanity of whoever believes him. Even though, the real problem in this claim, is that it removes the attention from all the other religious groups. David Icke is using the same tactic that Hitler, Stalin, and the Chinese Communists use, which is to distract the general public from truly seeing, identifying and knowing the perpetrators;

- Terrorizing — By systematically pushing an apocalyptical view on his listeners, David Icke is using the same tactic of the Vatican and the cult leaders, who seek to unite their followers under the same fears. Does he provide solutions to fight this terror that he insists about? No! On the contrary! As recent interviews, in 2020, to the London Real, show us, David Icke takes more pride in being right for the past decades than in seeing the world in a better state than he predicted. And it makes us wonder: Should a prophet be happy to see his world 'burn in flames' as he envisioned, or instead take pride on that what he envisioned didn't come to fruition, because he was able to change the future outcome in time? What kind of prophet should we truly follow? The one who wins his pride by being right without solutions, or the one who loses it by helping the world?

• Idolatry — The systematic use of the word Illuminati, doesn't depict the Power Elite as a bunch of criminals, but rather enlightened beings that know more than anyone else. What David Icke ends up doing with this type of speech, is actually promote such Elite, leading Freemasonry to become 'one of the most popular secret societies that ever existed'. As some of the leaders told me in person: — "We never had so many applications as now." And so, Icke is literally promoting the Power Elite while claiming to do the opposite. Many of the morons I have met in my life, tried to join freemasonry, precisely because of this Cinderella type of speech. They couldn't care less about numerology, or mysticism or spirituality. Most of the recent acquisitions in freemasonry are fulfilling the self-made prophecy of David Icke — people who lust for power.

Now, should we question ourselves and wonder if David Icke is a prophet, a conspiracist or a CIA agent? Because, he seems to be aware of the fact that people are too stupid to understand the complexity of the world in which they live, when he insists on creating a linear narrative and segregating one group as the bad guys, and which, by the way, is historically, a very British thing to do, either it is related to xenophobia or racism.

THE ANTICHRIST: THE GRAND PLAN OF TOTAL GLOBAL ENSLAVEMENT

Maybe, anytime soon, he will follow the historical practices of his own people, and suggest isolating the freemasons in concentration camps as well. Would that solve the problems of the world in his perspective?

Does anyone, in his right mind, believe that by murdering all the freemasons, the problems of the world would vanish? Because this is what it seems that David Icke is trying to say, when doing what he criticizes the most: treating people like dumb sheep!

For the past ten years of my life, I have met many of his most devoted followers, readers and believers, and came to the conclusion that they tend to be ignorant in a special kind of way. For they are so immersed in David Icke's beliefs, that they do not listen, do not learn, and insist on his narrative, that all the members of Secret Societies are blood-drinking alien-reptile shape-sifting worshippers trying to conquer the world.

Even if I wish not to say that David Icke is a liar and a manipulator of mass opinion, I have never met one of his followers that is not a fool, fed with so many lies, that there is nothing I can say, to make such person understand the truth.

Through the veil of informing the public, Icke is blinding them!

Is David Icke creating a special kind of stupid — another group of sheep? Because, you see, David Icke criticizes the white sheep, while he himself tries to be the shepherd of the black sheep — a bunch of people who believe to know the truth and, in fact, know nothing. They are now simply terrified of the world in which they live, and paranoid about any type of information, no matter how superficial it might be. They have been brainwashed with David Icke's views!

Is that a good thing? Is there a positive side in this?

Taking into consideration that the followers are still ignorant but misinformed, and consider Freemasonry to be the supreme religion of the world, I don't think so. Besides, I have caught David Icke on camera several times, referring himself to other religions, while purposely occulting their names. And I ask: Why does he promote Freemasonry so much but hides the names of other religious groups?

It makes one wonder about his intentions!

His over-simplistic view of reality makes nobody any favor! And, in most cases, what he says about religion, is completely wrong! But how can he know? How can a person without experience know anything? Where is his supposed 'research' coming from?

At least, Leo Lyon Zagami, who was a former member of various Secret Societies, and admits it publicly, reveals evidence that anyone can confirm, and explains himself without promoting groups and ideologies. David Icke does none of that! Icke promotes Freemasonry and looks like an agent of the Rothschild family.

The more he talks about the Queen of England, the more it seems that he works for the Rothschild. Because the Rothschild control England, not the Queen. The Queen is a symbolic distraction for the masses!

Chapter 45: How to Identify the False Prophets?

False prophets are cult-leaders who's mission is to distract, restrain and confuse.

David Icke fits this criteria! He has managed to create a cult-like following around him by using a type of speech based on fear, dogma and half-truths mixes with half-lies.

I am perfectly in agreement with his half-truths. The problem is in knowing which part of his speech is a half-lie. Because, as former Director of the CIA — Richard Helms — said, in regards to big lies, the story is "Incredible enough to be interesting".

We become so immersed in David Icke's story, that we forget to analyze what he says or come to the conclusion that most of it has no evidence whatsoever.

His speech is, fundamentally, based on assumptions, most of which I have found to be a lie.

This leads me to another observation that must be placed in the form of two questions:

- Why is David Icke promoting certain groups and downgrading others?

- Is he hiding his sources to subliminally proclaim himself above the general truth?

Before answering these questions, we must remind ourselves that people do change, and Icke has changed a lot over the years, adopting more and more of a narcissistic view of himself. Which doesn't tell us that he was or wasn't a different person before.

We can, however, and at the very least, say this and very clearly:

- He is a bad reporter;

- He promotes Freemasonry;

- And he, subliminally, creates an idolatry around the Power Elite, in a similar way as Vorilhon — founder of Raelism —, even though following a different route.

I can't really give him more credit than that, taking into consideration that his public presentations are based on slides with quotes, seemingly for entertainment purposes, and present close to zero information that can be verified and confirmed.

He could be called, in essence, a motivational speaker, except that he doesn't motivate. He terrorizes! And we should always suspect those who use the tactics mentioned here! And as much as we can only trust those who don't! Namely, William Cooper, who was murdered by the CIA, and warned us about this, saying on his radio show — The Hour of the Time:

"David Icke is one of the biggest liars and disinformation artists that ever lived! He claims that the Global Elite are human reptiles shape-shifters, with no evidence to prove it! He poisons the truth with a lot of fear mongering and self-made fables!"

The first time that David Icke appeared on public television, he proclaimed to be the son of God. Nothing wrong with that! We all are! But the questions we must ask, taking into consideration his attitude, are:

- Could he be unconscious of what he is doing to a certain level, or just be another victim of the CIA MK-Ultra project?

- And, if he is conscious, why is he not doing a proper research work, like any other reporter, and providing us with sources to confirm what he says?

William Cooper explained to us why, in a recorded speech, in which he said that, "If you don't understand the nature of your enemy, and the weapons they use, you cannot fight that enemy! You can't fight the battle, and you shouldn't even be in the battlefield! And that is why you are losing the war!"

THE ANTICHRIST: THE GRAND PLAN OF TOTAL GLOBAL ENSLAVEMENT

The following words of William Cooper are extremely important, as not only they discredit David Icke and others like him, but also show us the importance of knowing how to identify the ones who truly want to help mankind. He said:

"Don't spread a rumor! Spread the truth! Document it and prove it! Make it irrefutable and you too will become dangerous to those who enslave us! You don't really understand what a terrible burden it is to try to wake people up and find out that they have walls built in front of them! They want to be slaves!"

What Cooper was trying to tell us, is that we must understand that, uncovering the truth, requires facts that can be confirmed and not just assumptions. We must be aware of those who spread conspiracies as a form of distraction.

This is why the efforts put into this book and these words, are based on the same beliefs of William Miltom Cooper, when he said:

"Read about everything, listen to everyone, but don't believe in anything unless you can prove it with your own research!"

If someone can't prove his claims, and is focusing on a narrative that intends to intimidate and generalize groups of people, rather that identify precise events, then this person is taking advantage of the fact that the masses are too unaware of the importance of rationalizing what they hear, which is the same as to control them by discrediting them. Thanks to David Icke, most conspiracists are now viewed as a bunch of lunatics who believe the Queen of England is a lizard controlling the world.

Even if the Queen of England is a lizard, or a giant butterfly, or a demon with three heads, the main point is that she doesn't control anything — The Rothschild do! And so do the Rockefeller, through their own foundation! Both of which are in control of health, education, finance, and the many wars we witnessed, at least, for more than a hundred years.

Nearly all of the Secret Groups gathering the most powerful individuals in the world, where founded by the Rockefeller Family, namely, The Bilderberg, The Committee of 300, and the Trilateral Commission.

Even the Gates Foundation has associated with the Rockefeller Foundation in his ID2020 project, which intends to impose mandatory vaccination and microchip the world population.

Why aren't these so-called prophets, warning us about these facts, instead of talking about walking lizards?

Chapter 46: Religious Atheism and Spiritual Prostitution.

One of the techniques that many of the new age prophets seem to demonstrate to have, and that attracts people in like flies to a blue light, is the ability to hypnotize under the veil of being open-minded and wanting free love.

The many prophets that are appearing in the world, seem to, one way or another, all converge towards what Raelism portrays — free love without judgements. And that is why Raelism represents the religion that the Elite wishes the common people to have. It is perfectly aligned with their agenda.

Raelism, which is based on Fundamentalism and Realism, and promoted as an extraterrestrial pseudo-religious idea, is another project of mass control, and consists on trying to convince people to reject their spirituality under the veil of religion.

Through these different branches of religious imbecility, the CIA is able to analyze mass behavior and take the Jim Jones project to a whole new level, even though following the same ideology — Communism and Atheism hidden behind the cover or idolatry. Not so different from what we have seen in the past decades in North Korea!

As a matter of fact, the combination of religion with monarchy and politics, has always been an ambition of all Elites throughout history.

The ultimate goal of these groups is to bring forth the idea that there is no other religion but the Government.

This is why the Raelian Movement fits the agenda of the Elites in many points, namely:

- Promiscuity — The idea that both family and marriage are irrelevant, and sexual promiscuity is more important than love. In fact, in a public speech filmed for their own social media channel, Vorilhon confirmed this by saying that, "Love is an illusion";

- Technocracy — The idea that science is above spirituality, and that cloning and Genetically Modified Organisms are acceptable, which certainly puts the Rockefeller Foundation and the Monsanto Company at the top of the pyramid of power. And I wouldn't be surprised if these companies were feeding the Swiss bank account of Vorilhon;

- Immorality — By classifying everything as an 'illusion', the movement succeeds in promoting immorality as morality, therefore inducing the acceptance of immoral acts. It is then not shocking to see that the group attracts brainwashed individuals seeking for easy sex and social acceptance without moral judgements.

Now, how could a lunatic want to create such a religion based on lies, and still get a large following, as well as the funds necessary to proceed with his ideas?

In order for you to answer this question, while seeing the pertinence of asking it, when analyzing this and other popular religious groups, you need to look at it from two angles — the leader and those behind it. For both have motivations of their own!

As we have seen, the movement fits into the agenda of the Elites, so their funding may very well be proportional to the size of their following. Either way, they provide a fertile ground for studies, like a bunch of lab rats.

As for the leader — Claude Vorilhon —, he has expressed his intent clearly, when a reporter, from Quebec's TQS Television Network, asked him, in 2002, if he was having sex with all of his followers, and he answered while laughing:

— "Unfortunately, I did not sleep with all. However, I wish I could have sex 50 times a day. I am always interested in women who come to me with love."

In other words, it is a cult created by a middle-age man to justify having sex with plenty of young girls. A fact confirmed by an anonymous source and former member, named Corinne F., on French Television, and who said that, "He removes guilt feelings from people that have incestuous or pedophilic tendencies".

THE ANTICHRIST: THE GRAND PLAN OF TOTAL GLOBAL ENSLAVEMENT

As the same reporters showed, many pamphlets shared by the Raelian Movement clearly indicate to welcome pedophilic traits, or at least, not condemn them. Which explains why several Raelians have been convicted of pedophilia in 2001.

In 1992, an ex-Raëlist also went to major media outlets to accuse Vorilhon and the other Raëlists of participating in pedophilia and child-sacrifice.

Although most of the accusations were suppressed and never proven, the techniques used by the Movement to attract and seduce the perverts of society, have been confirmed by Claude Vorilhon himself, in a phone interview he made in 1995, when saying:

— "We put the prettiest girls in the front and the ugliest, the fat and ugly, in the back."

Sage Ali, who was a member of the movement for 17 years, said in a testimony that, "Sexuality forms an important part of Raëlian doctrine, which promotes liberal views of sexuality, including homosexuality, bisexuality, polyamory, masturbation and prostitution. Raëlian spiritual practices include sensual meditation, which involves ritual stimulation of erogenous zones. Raëlians also practice naturism and are advocates of toplessness in females."

Since all of Raël's Order of Angels have consented and are committed to 'Service the Messiah sensually', lesbianism among them is actively promoted and the better to join together 'to enhance the Prophet's pleasure'. According to Brigitte Boisselier, coordinator for the Order of Angels, "Freedom of love is freedom to say yes to many lovers." And so, prostitutes, nymphomaniacs, as well as pornstars, and anyone else who might be addicted to sex and promiscuity, finally can have a religion of their own.

One would think that all this evidence could be enough to discredit the madman behind the movement, and yet, the movement he created in Auvergne, France, in 1974, claims to have 100 thousand followers in 2020 and from around the globe.

The movement is based on a lie, but who cares about the truth when morality goes out the window and one is free to participate in orgies?

This seems to be the ultimate goal of the group, as many parties of the movement show. In simple terms, Raelism can be resumed to the promotion of prostitution and atheism.

Satanism would be a better concept for this religion, but even Satanists seem far more shy and morally orientated than the Raelians wish to be.

Raelism is indeed the religion that the Elite want for the common people — religious stupidity based on copy-pasted ideas and suppressed spirituality — as well as suppressed consciousness — through perversion and sexual obsession.

Why worship a God when you can worship a group of humans?

The main problem here, is that the Elite is that group.

Chapter 47: The Suppression of Mass Consciousness.

Unfortunately, human beings haven't learned to separate the knowledge from the reputation of an organization or its leader, and so, much of the information that is valuable to raise awareness, and truly create an enlightening civilization, is either ignored, or hidden, discredited and suppressed.

The biggest revolutions mankind witnesses, and many of the world wars, and the constant fights for power, are still demonstrations of madness, greed and ignorance.

The symbols behind these events, may always be the same, but we must not be confused by this, as religion keeps dividing itself in branches that reinterpret the knowledge differently, while starting a new system of values under a different name.

Some movements end up becoming more famous than others, but they're just like different religions following the exact same truth from, sometimes, completely different perspectives, or putting great efforts to avoid it.

Any perversion of the knowledge within such groups is of the sole responsibility of their leaders and founders.

Another aspect worth mentioning is that, many current Secret Societies, in order to achieve more power and influence, invite individuals from already powerful and rich families, or with great influence over the masses, such as artists and politicians, to join them. This strategy of expansion made them forget moral and ethical values, in order to increase their competitive leverage among themselves, and that's why we now associate them with evil, war, politics and oppression, although only a minority of individuals is responsible for this and the rest is predominantly good and truly more kind and wise than the majority of the population, with or without religious beliefs.

In fact, most religions have a strong tendency to satisfy the urges of the masses, the most strong impulses, and are not necessarily more popular because they are more truthful. The correlation between success, truth and power, is another illusion in which many fall — seduced by the desires of the members.

The world has descended into such a need for narcissistic satisfaction, that most religious groups now tend to attract members in order to satisfy their needs, either emotional, sexual, financial, social, or intellectual. These members then close the eyes to all the rest, and abstain from criticizing or questioning, because they want to enjoy such privileges. And yet, it is obvious, by the character of the majority in any group, what attracted them to such group.

On the other hand, as the gap between normality and abnormality, as well as the intellectual and financial gap in society keep increasing, religions tend to be more radical in order to satisfy their followers, and leaving them to face an hostile world in isolation is usually not an option for many of them.

The truth is that there isn't a cure for the lack of awareness of our condition, and feeling bad about ourselves reflects the evidence that there's something terribly wrong with this world and the way it affects our personal reality.

Meanwhile, "none are so hopelessly enslaved as those who falsely believe they are free" (Johann Wolfgang Von Goethe, Freemason). For nobody can escape this network, which has grown in influence and is gradually introducing us to transhumanism.

Those who try it, are condemned to failure and rejection by society. And truly, "in a time of universal deceit, telling the truth is a revolutionary act" (George Orwell, Freemason).

Chapter 48: The Challenge in Being Oneself.

The big lie starts early in school, when the most creative are often labeled with ADHD (Attention Deficit Hyperactivity Disorder) and then medicated with Ritalin, a drug containing more fluoride than any other common antidepressant (94%).

By the time one reaches adulthood, the ability to rationalize and make proper decisions is no longer available as it should be in a normal human being. Most will simply 'go with the flow' and succumb to the normal of their environment.

There's clearly a war against consciousness happening, and the most resistant fighters are the chosen victims, in a deliberate, persistent and consistent dumbing down of the population.

Choosing to be free is now a painful process, by which one faces discrimination, bullying and isolation. And, if the Rothschild family is in control of the physical aspect of the world — namely, through governments and finance — then, it is the Rockefeller family that appears to be in control of the mental and emotional aspects.

Any research on the topic of mental health leads us to the Rockefeller Foundation, which seems to be doing the work of the Rothschild through the mind control of the population. And they, coincidentally, also seem to have the most investments in the profiting from psychotropics and the Pharmaceutical Industry as a global business.

Dr. Ewen Cameron, who was President of the American Psychiatric Association in 1952, affirmed these goals in a public speech, when mentioning that, "What we call morals, are simply the customs, prohibitions and rules which a society maintains at any given time... The United Nations Organization deserves the support of all who are concerned with the building of a New World Order... There can be only one education anywhere on the Earth and that is education for world citizenship."

Then, in 1953, Dr. Ewen Cameron, wrote that, "The subject which will be of most importance politically is mass psychology... Although this science will be diligently studied, it will be rigidly confined to the governing class. The populace will not be allowed to know how its convictions were generated."

He was referring here to the engineering of a mass belief-system. Which leads us to a common assumption that the ignorant tend to affirm in regards to themselves: "I cannot be manipulated because I make my own decisions."

Most people are so unconscious of their own behaviors, that they can't see themselves systematically falling into the idea of "social acceptance" and "trends" as being the absorption of an ideology that promotes degradation and humiliation, or quite simply, enslavement to social ideals.

In today's world, a big percentage of women are nothing but common prostitutes, who have exchanged their biological need to have a family of their own, for the idea that promiscuity, a cat to sleep with at night, and a highly paid job, will increase their social worth, status and self-esteem. Many of these women grow old, lonely and miserable, and can't see why, because they have been programmed to do such mistakes, and to pursue a falsehood. The lies are then operating like a blindfold that stops them from introspecting and changing.

They will react violently to anyone who tries to awaken them as well!

The ridicule of men by the media, on the other hand, convinced them that they are somehow inferior to women, and that opposing women would make them misogynist. As such, the overall humiliation of men, has indeed led them to forming dissenting groups such as the so-called INCELS (Involuntary Celibates) or MGTOW (Men Going Their Own Way), and which are basically growing numbers of men who refuse to cooperate with the system and are then discriminated, opposed and ridiculed by society as a whole — a brainwashed society.

THE ANTICHRIST: THE GRAND PLAN OF TOTAL GLOBAL ENSLAVEMENT

Most importantly, this type of discrimination, is making sure that only the men who cope with the degrading behaviors of their women are allowed to procreate and create the next generation for humanity — a certainly much more obedient and degrading generation than the extremely weak we see today.

In doing this, the Elite systematically increases the gap between them and the masses.

The new ideal woman is a whore who undresses herself on social media, and the new ideal man is a kind of hermaphrodite without any capacity to speak for himself and without any will of his own, except when enslaving himself to his woman, and therefore having a personal will subjugated to the will of a female, and as an extension of hers.

In this idealization of society, women downgrade themselves and men, as potential leaders, are eliminated.

In 2018, Dr. Bobbi Wegner — Professor at the Harvard Graduate School of Education in Human Development and Psychology — actually said, in a public Ted talk, that, "Feminist boys are our future men".

This idea is typically disguised under the premise of equality between genders. But any scientific study that supports it is accepted, while any other that discredits the possibility is rejected.

Science is then seen as a form of religion that must match the ideology dictated from above.

As Dr. Shiva said in an interview (2020): "The modern priesthood aren't in churches but in universities! They manipulate, not educate!"

Chapter 49: The Great Scam of the Psychiatric Industry.

In 1970, a joint strategy outlined by the mental heath industry and the pharmaceutical industry was already obvious.

This strategy started with the labelling of psychiatric disorders — either of an emotional or behavioral nature — to any predisposition that didn't fit the system.

They would then call them 'brain diseases' in order to claim the origin as being a 'chemical imbalance'. This way, they could then launch a propaganda campaign, so intense and persistent that the public would soon believe in nothing but pills — chemical balancers for chemical imbalances.

This was a well-planned scam that persists today, despite no known scientific evidence proving that there is a correlation between the two topics. Psychiatry become part of a triangle of control that includes the globalist agenda and the pharmaceutical lobbies — the interconnection between the Rothschild, the Rockefeller and the Psychiatric Industry towards the same goal.

This triangle then became the weapon by which the political, the medical and the pharmaceutical are aligned. Psychology, marketing campaigns, social engineering, industrial drugs, psychotropic drugs, all become branches of the same agenda.

Among such drugs, one of the most popular chemicals to dumb down the population is aspartame. It is found in many drinks and other products. This FDA approved chemical, is, according to Dr. James D. Bowen, "A brainwashing agent. You lose your ability to think independently and effectively, or to realistically challenge anything".

A person that vehemently opposed this attack on global consciousness through the use of psychiatry and drugs, was L. Ron Hubbard — Founder of Scientology. He used to easily unveil their scams in his lectures, most of which where recorded and became part of the studying of his followers.

The whole purpose of Scientology was to do the opposite, and lead people to a higher consciousness, through their own mental health therapeutical methods. As such, as soon as Scientology started, in the 1950s, there was an immediate campaign put in place to discredit it.

The reason for this opposition was, according to Hubbard, due to Scientology's opposition to psychiatric practices i.e., the use of psycho-surgery (lobotomy and electric-shock), psychotropic drugs, psychopolitics, and the exposure of different mind control methods.

According to Hubbard, "Psychiatry and Mental Health were chosen as a vehicle to undermine and destroy the west, and Scientology stood in their way.... They have infiltrated boards of education, the armed services, even the churches".

Former Scientologist, Ingo Swann, confirmed this. He wrote in his books that there are many techniques in Scientology that were and still are of extreme value to the Intelligence Community, for whom he worked for many years. He also said that many different groups were trying to seize Scientology, namely, Psychiatrists, Freemasons, The Pharmaceutical Lobbies, and the CIA.

The purpose of these different lobbies was to present new discoveries in their field as if being the result of their own research. Reason why, over the years, Psychiatry seems to present more and more so-called "new discoveries" that resemble what is already known in Scientology for many decades, and this, while discrediting and attacking Scientologists.

Chapter 50: A Circus of Clowns Named Scientology.

In TV shows and News about Scientology, we can see Scientology's enemies on both sides — the critics as well as the public relations of Scientology — playing with words. And we wonder why no one is there to defend Scientology effectively. And the reason why, is that this is a show made to dissuade the general public from joining in, and while all the information is being stolen by Secret Intelligence Agencies.

The Psychiatric Industry also wanted control over the activities of the CCHR — Citizens Commission on Human Rights. And they do have it now! The anti-Psychiatry publications, financed by the International Association of Scientologists, stay in the smallest circles of Scientologists, and are rarely distributed in the public. In doing this, they managed to prevent the general public from knowing how the drugs promoted by the Psychiatric Industry and the Pharmaceutical Industry affect them physically and mentally.

The Association's patrons in Scientology believe that something effective was done with their money, and don't realize that the brochures are usually not distributed outside Scientology. An effective hit against Psychiatry would have been the publication in the internet of these brochures, but that never happened.

The same applies to any complain in regards to the abuses of Scientologists and their own violations of the Churches' ethics. They do have a special section to deal with these matters. But they never do! They also have books, written by the founder, that clearly outline procedures and the correction of behaviors when such procedures aren't followed. But that is ignored as well!

One can then ask: Why aren't Scientologists acting like Scientologists and following their own books, procedures and ethical codes?

Most of the so-called Sea Org Members — Higher rank in Scientology — typically know nothing about the most basic teachings of the founder and do the most absurd mistakes. How is that possible?

Scientologists, today, constantly violate their own ethics' books, and ignore any interference — from both the outside and even inside the group — that attempts to show them that. Such attempts are viewed as attacks on Scientology, and fought violently!

Scientologists — both online and offline — constantly insult, offend and see as fit to persecute anyone who attempts at making them look at their own immoral behavior — despite the fact that most of such behavior goes against Scientology itself and is clarified openly in their own books.

In 2019, a report was sent to the Headquarters of Scientology in Europe, in regards to the abuses and constant violations of a representative of Scientology in Lithuania, named Jurgita Braskute. The report intended to expose these violations in regards to a friend of mine, who had joined for several basic courses in the Organization.

The purpose of my friend was to improve herself, her life, and her relationship with her boyfriend and coworkers. But Braskute, instead of applying a personality and mental health test — created by the founder to diagnose each person individually, and then recommend the ideal study materials —, systematically tried to sell different courses, most of which were useless and unrelated to anything that my friend needed and wanted to study, and then focused on making her spend as much money as possible rather than seeing or testing results.

In fact, one of the complains my friend often made, was that Braskute never answered any questions and never corrected any doubts. She would ignore everything!

As for the so-called courses, they included no more than reading a few pamphlets of about 20 pages — expanded with several images and meaningless exercises, not to seem like actually only 4 pages length of information in average — on common sense, for €20 to €30 euros each.

As if that wasn't enough, Braskute started recommending my friend that she should abandon her boyfriend, and join the Organization, working for her in Lithuania.

THE ANTICHRIST: THE GRAND PLAN OF TOTAL GLOBAL ENSLAVEMENT

In order to accomplish her goals, Braskute did what in Scientology is called 'playing the 3rd party' — putting two people against each other based on the creation of self-doubt and the undermining of a relationship with lies. Braskute literally used the knowledge in Scientology to destroy a relationship, extort as much money as possible from a person, and then manipulate her into joining the Organization, working for free — which is also known as slave labor.

According to the conversations that I verified (when conducted online), Braskute was suggesting my friend that 'maybe she does not want to be with her boyfriend', 'maybe she is confused about the relationship', 'maybe she needs more data before deciding what she wants in life', and that 'maybe her boyfriend is not interested in her well-being'.

I confronted Braskute myself, in a one-on-one interview about these behaviors, and she lied to my face in all the questions asked. But this constant invalidation and manipulation of a person's will against her own interest, that Braskute was using, is called gaslighting. It's a tactic commonly used by narcissists to invalidate a person's sanity and suppress individual will.

In the Church of Scientology, they call this a 1.1 behavior — on a scale that goes from -40 to +40, and which, accordingly, places artists, musicians and writers between +20 and +40.

Taking into consideration that I am an author, a musician and a painter, by attacking me and discrediting me, and lying to my face, with 1.1. behaviors, Braskute was essentially attacking everything that Scientology represents.

Chapter 51: Why Do Scientologists Act Like Criminals?

Why was a National Representative of Scientology in Lithuania, named Jurgita Braskute, using Scientology to destroy a relationship, manipulate a person, suppress her mental health, and extort money from her for three consecutive years — between 2017 and 2019?

Why was Jurgita Braskute using Scientology to actually do evil and drive someone insane? To be able to extort even more money from her and convince her to work for Scientology for free, once the relationship was over and her personal life was destroyed? To create co-dependency, as narcissists typically do? How is that even possible? How can Scientologists use what they know about evil, mind control and narcissism, to actually use it for their own goals? And why was that allowed by the Headquarters?

Braskute did something else, two actions that are totally absurd according to the principles of Scientology:

- She ignored the fact that my friend consumed drugs, as if that was perfectly acceptable:

- And Braskute also refused to audit my friend, which is the therapeutical procedure created by the founder to improve mental health and raise consciousness, e.g., the whole purpose as to why Scientology was created.

On the other hand, why would Braskute do that, if then it wouldn't be possible to continue with the gaslighting and the mind control techniques? And why wasn't she expelled from the Church for, basically, acting against the Church?

Moreover, another thing that Braskute did, to maintain control over her new found victim, was to keep her isolated and distant from other Scientologists, so that they had no chance of questioning Braskute's actions — a clear evidence that she knew what she was doing, and that she knew it was a crime and a violation against the Church.

I communicated this situation with the Headquarters of Scientology, who where quick to indicate that this was a complete violation of their own laws. They asked me to send a report in order to investigate.

This report, with several pages and evidence, including tests made to my friend, was sent to the Headquarters — The Sea Organization —, but the investigations were dropped and never truly applied.

Several requests were made to the Headquarters, asking for a follow up on the situation, but the only thing Scientologists did was promise an investigation that never really occurred.

I then communicated the case with other high ranked and independent Scientologists, who explained that the Headquarters of Scientology refuses to investigate their own staff, no matter how many crimes they may commit, against Scientology or its members, or even society itself. It is the new policy of Scientology not to investigate itself. They are in the business of wrecking lives and extorting money from people, not helping them!

Following this case, another Scientologist called me, and asked many personal questions — namely, about my job and my salary —, trying to convince me to do a course, which according to her, was for my own well-being — that course would cost over five thousand dollars.

One would think that Scientologists are in the business of making people better. That isn't the case! Braskute used the knowledge of Scientology to extort money, gaslight and use mind control techniques on a person. Those at the top of the Organization, protected and defended such behaviors and didn't investigate them, despite being a clear violation of their own ethics. On the contrary, they used the problem to their own advantage, by later trying to extort more money.

Braskute succeeded in destroying the relationship of my friend, and leaving her as lost as always, and as addicted to drugs as she had been before joining Scientology. But they did not succeed in getting the five thousand dollars from me.

Chapter 52. Why Scientology Only Wants Your Money?

On the surface, Scientology seems to be working as always, but in fact, it is being suppressed from the inside.

There are many powerful lobbies interested in the technology developed by Ron Hubbard but that, at the same time, don't want the general public to access it. And so, they use the Organization for their own ends, while discrediting it for the majority of the population, and by creating prices so high that make the Church inaccessible to the masses.

This strategy has been working well! For I have never met anyone who wants to read a book written by L. Ron Hubbard, even when I tell them that they don't need to join Scientology to read such book.

Most people are also not willing to pay so much for their so-called courses, and that don't contain not even half the information of the original ones anymore.

In this game, David Miscavige is just a mini-Napoleon, who doesn't dare go amongst Scientologists without his bodyguards. But he does get the entire profit that the Church makes all around the world.

According to the Free Scientologists Organization (an independent organization created by dissents of Scientology), "The Enslavers are largely in control of planet Earth and they are not going to just sit and watch the Church of Scientology make free spiritual beings without doing something to stop it".

Today, Scientology is based on what is called 'donations' to avoid being taxed, while nothing is accessed and studied without significant costs. And yet, Scientology is actually a Corporation. And most of the materials, have been so violated and altered, that the vast majority is nothing but common sense to which new members pay large sums of money to access and read.

You may also assume that, within this massive conspiracy of ignorance, Scientologists are friends to one another, but that only applies for as long as you are serving and feeding the Scientology Corporation Beast with your money and time, e.g., studying or working as a volunteer.

Scientologists are now so enslaved by what they call "games", that without their commissions, they have nothing. Most Scientologists live in poverty, despite what they have to charge for their courses and materials. All the money goes to David Miscavige and his partners.

Chapter 53. Religions are Corporations!

In today's world, no religion is trustworthy anymore! And the prove of this, is that, as soon as you start to think and ask questions, nobody likes you anymore. In particular, being a good writer is incompatible with any religion.

That is why many have rejected me in some way or another, for asking too many questions and rejecting their totally 'Idiocratic Beliefs', or by simply confronting them with their lack of ethics and violations against their own principles — as was the case of the report I sent to the Headquarters of Scientology, and that was ignored.

This said, to believe that Scientology is a cult, is to neglect the fact that all religions in today's world are, in fact, cults. And to believe that Scientology is a Religion, and not a Corporation, is to ignore the fact that, in today's world, all religions are also Corporations.

They all have to pay something to someone! They all have to be funded by powerful individuals! And none survives on donations alone!

This idea, that Churches depend on charity only, is a fantasy in which many want to believe but doesn't correspond to the facts any longer.

Several respected and long term members of the Jehovah Witnesses even stopped talking to me, when I exposed this fantasy to them, and showed that Chase Bank funds the Jehovah Witnesses, and Chase Bank is owned by the Rockefeller Family. Which means they are agents of those they think they are opposing — the warlords and Satanists of their own magazines.

According to Wikipedia, "Chase Bank is closely associated with and has financed the oil industry, having longstanding connections with its board of directors to the successor companies of Standard Oil, especially ExxonMobil, which are also Rockefeller holdings... Under the leadership of David Rockefeller, the bank became part of a bank holding company, the Chase Manhattan Corporation."

You would think men and women with over 40, 50 or 70yo could look at the facts and accept them. Instead, they runaway like little children when hearing for the first time that candy is bad for the teeth, Santa isn't real and fairies don't leave money under the pillow at night.

People can't handle the truth!

Chapter 54. When Satan Pays for Your Bible!

Barbara G. Harrison investigated the Jehovah Witnesses and said (In her book, 'Visions of Glory: A History and a Memory of Jehovah's Witnesses', 1978), "Financial reports are never published (at least, not in the United States). Calls from reporters, researchers, state senators inquiring into the finances of the Society go unanswered... The Society's attorneys refuse to answer requests for information. The Society's Bank of record, Chase Manhattan, likewise gives away no secrets.

Rank-and-file Witnesses believe absolutely that the Society's stewardship is beyond reproach; they ask no questions. To question the Lord's 'governing body', they are told, is to doubt the Lord Himself!"

It is interesting to notice, however, that Chase Bank — the Jehovah's Witnesses Bank — has a history of evil and corruption, the same evil and corruption they seem to condemn and oppose in their Church.

Doesn't that matter, or are the freely offered bibles more important than the truth? It doesn't matter that Satan, himself, is sponsoring the bibles of the Jehovah Witnesses?

Isn't that a huge hypocrisy, to talk bad about the ones paying for their own existence?

According to a press release, from the National Archives and Record Administration (NARA) in 2004, Chase Bank has aided the Nazis and Nazi sympathizers during World War II, through different transactions, allowing the purchase of Marks (Hitler's currency) with dollars at a discounted rate, while blocking transactions that came mainly from Jews who had fled Germany.

In other words, and according to Wikipedia, "Nazi Germany was able to offer these Marks below face-value because they had been stolen from émigrés fleeing the Nazi regime.

Between 1936 and 1941, the Nazis amassed over $20 million, and the businesses enabling these transactions earned $1.2 million in commissions. Of these commissions, over $500,000 went to Chase National Bank and its subagents."

These facts were discovered when the FBI began its investigation in October 1940... However, Chase National Bank's executives were never federally prosecuted because Chase's lead attorney threatened to reveal FBI, Army, and Navy "sources and methods" in court... To avoid such revelations,... they were never prosecuted.

Besides the controversial Rückwanderer Mark Scheme, NARA records also revealed another controversy during the occupation of France by the Nazis. From the late 1930s until June 14, 1941, when President Franklin D. Roosevelt issued an Executive Order freezing German assets, Chase National Bank worked with the Nazi government.

The order blocking any access to French accounts in the U.S. by anyone, but especially by the Nazis was issued by Secretary of the Treasury, Henry Morgenthau Jr., with the approval of Roosevelt. Within hours of the order, however, Chase unblocked the accounts and the funds were transferred through South America to Nazi Germany.

In recent controversies, revealed on Wikipedia, it is said that, "The U.S. Treasury's Office of Foreign Assets Control found that JPMorgan had illegally aided dictatorships in Cuba, Sudan, Liberia and Iran, including transferring 32,000 ounces of gold bullion (valued at approximately $20,560,000) to the benefit of a bank in Iran."

Now, isn't it interesting, that the Jehovah Witnesses preach against the powers of Satan, against dictatorships, while Satan is sponsoring their religion and paying for their brochures about the Armageddon? I personally find that very interesting!

Imagine walking around with a book paid by your enemy while slandering his name! That is what the Jehovah Witnesses do when slandering Satan!

THE ANTICHRIST: THE GRAND PLAN OF TOTAL GLOBAL ENSLAVEMENT

Sadly, the members of the Jehovah Witnesses, a bunch of cynical and hypocrites, are too arrogant and deluded by their child-like fantasies to accept such facts.

Chapter 55: The Infiltration of Religious Organizations.

Despite all the facts exposed, we must also acknowledge the difference between religions who started with lies and those who were infiltrated and corrupted from the inside.

It is usually neglected that many religions were hijacked by individuals with personal motives, and what exactly occurred during such period — a scenario that always seems very familiar to the drama and treason portrayed by many Hollywood movies.

As an example, we have the Church of Scientology, often criticized through a scapegoat — the founder, L. Ron Hubbard. For nobody seems to be smart enough to realize that the Church of Scientology is, in fact, and since 1986, the Church of David Miscavige — a self-appointed leader, owner and authority for life.

Many Scientologists who were expelled, accused him of several crimes, and wrote reports about it. In one of those reports, from May 1984 — two years before he took office — The Scientology Committee of Evidence of Los Angeles, California, declared David Miscavige a Suppressive Person (Scientology's technical word for criminal) due to activities that intended to suppress Scientology and Scientologists, and judged him a traitor of the organization.

This report was signed by the Chairman, Vincent Barnes, and other members of the board, namely, Joyce Barnes, Ron Lowley, and Mel Smith, and was endorsed by Capt. W.B. Robertson — Chairman of the OT Committee (one of the highest sections in Scientology, and responsible for providing the highest levels of the Organization).

Among the many crimes of which David Miscavige was found guilty, we find:

- Persuading others to resist authority and revolt against the hierarchy of the Church of Scientology through mutiny, and by engaging in malicious rumor-mongering to destroy the authority of higher officers or leading names of Scientology;

- Organizing a splinter group, which takes and perverts Scientology materials and practices, though an Organization that David Miscavige, together with additional six staff members (self-entitled "Company founders" and "trustees"), registered as a Company in California — The Religious Technology Center (RTC) — without any written permission of the founder or a written policy from within the church;

- Making public statements against Scientology or Scientologists, and labeling Mission Holders as criminals;

- Violently attacking and punching several Scientologists during the investigations, and in the presence of others — John Aczel, Roger Barnes and Steve Warren;

- Receiving money, favors and encouragements to suppress Scientology or Scientologists.

David Miscavige organized his own committee, seeking to splinter off an area of Scientology and deny its properly constituted authority for personal profit, personal power, and, according to him, "save the organization from the higher officers of Scientology", while labeling all the Scientologists who opposed this as being opposed to Scientology.

During this period, David Miscavige also legally pursued scientologists (through his own recently founded Corporation — RTC). A behavior that the founder, himself, warned about as being suppressive to the Church.

THE ANTICHRIST: THE GRAND PLAN OF TOTAL GLOBAL ENSLAVEMENT

L. Ron Hubbard wrote that, "Everyone who spreads around libelous comments and evil slender about the alleged behavior of Clears (Scientology's technical word for OTs or most trained members) should be declared a Suppressive Person. Investigations should look for a criminal background of the person who spreads around such rumors" (In HCO PL 4.,1966).

David Miscavige was indeed committing crimes, and with outside help too. For the same report states that he was found to be an accomplice to the falsification of Hubbard's signature on legal documents. And this, despite a written last will of the founder, clearly attributing authority over the Church of Scientology to his wife — Mary Sue Hubbard.

In July 1981, Miscavige used falsified letters of Church attorneys to remove Mary Sue from her post as Controller.

A month prior to that, in June 1981, Miscavige removed his senior, Diane Voegeding, with a falsified message of Ron Hubbard.

According to the report, David Miscavige continued to remove staff members using false letters, until everyone at the top had been replaced.

Chapter 56: The Best Kept Secret in Scientology.

The main enemy of Scientology has always been in front of the eyes of the Scientologists, and it's David Miscavige himself.

Irmgard Wassard — graphologist and member of the Danish Graphological Society —, was presented with two original signatures of L. Ron Hubbard (from the 70s) and two other signatures for comparison, which were presented by David Miscavige. And after thorough examination of all four signatures, she explains that the two latest signatures (from 1982) were done by the same person and that this person is not identical with the one who signed with his name on the first two documents, since the questionable signatures show a variety of differences when compared to the authentic writing, and which is typical for forgeries.

Diana Voegeding (one of the former Scientologists that David Miscavige removed from office using falsified documents) explains, in a written and testified report, that David Miscavige, in exercising the activity as Californian Public Notary, received signatures signed by L. Ron Hubbard in the absence of L. Ron Hubbard being there, which is an offense against his status as Public Notary and forgery per the Californian law.

David Miscavige didn't just break the law and conspired to destroy Scientology. He also made sure nobody would ever know the truth. Miscavige did this by using the Secret Intelligence and private detectives to harass and arrest his opponents.

David Mayo, a former top Scientologist, was the person in charge of the accuracy of the Church scripture, and spent 25 years in the Church of Scientology, making him one of the most experienced individuals to have served in the Organization. As such, he was deemed a threat to David Miscavige.

On August 4, 1994, the Miscavige Cult of Scientology, utilized INTERPOL, the US DEA (Drug Enforcement Agency), and the DNCD (Dominican Nacional Control de Drogas) engaged in a ploy to descend on David Mayo to get him jailed by false allegations.

At the direction of David Miscaviage, David Mayo's home was surrounded by armed police, military and DNCD agents. David Mayo was handcuffed and the home was searched for fire arms, drugs and money.

No drugs or firearms were found. Nonetheless, David Mayo was taken to two police stations and eventually taken to Santo Domingo, where he was put in prison with no charges, explanation or reason.

David wasn't allowed to make a phone call to anyone — not even to a lawyer, to his wife Julie or to the American Embassy. That night, he was put in a small cell, stuffed with twelve other men overnight, in abhorrent conditions.

The next day, David Mayo learned that it was INTERPOL that was investigating him at the request of Scientology. And, eventually, he was released without being charged. But the incident was shockingly unexpected and intimidating, and the harassment didn't end there.

How could David Miscavige use INTERPOL and false allegations on a former member of the Religion, unless he had connections with high ranks in the Intelligence Community?

The only possibility for this to happen, is if Scientology was now another branch of the Shadow Government. But could it be possible that David Miscavige had been recruited by the CIA to be an infiltrated agent and hijack the Organization for the purposes of the Power Elite?

Chapter 57: Why the CIA Wants Scientology?

Scientology had been a long term enemy of Psychiatry, and therefore of the Rockefeller family and their mind control operations aided by the CIA, about which the founder had warned about multiple times.

In 'The Secret History of the CIA', authored by Joseph Trento, and based on an interview to former Vice Director of the CIA Clandestine Operations, Robert Trumbull Crowley, and shortly before he died, the name of David Miscavige appears as being among the CIA sources for projects like MK-ULTRA.

A source is not a paid agent but an individual who can occupy a position of influence, such as an international banker, a member of the print or television media, or a scholar or academic, who might be in a position to influence official decisions or supply necessary support for an official CIA position.

The information in the book didn't just provide the names of the sources, but also their address. And the building of the Religious Technology Center — founded by David Miscavige — is exactly on the address mentioned: 6331 Hollywood Blvd., Log Angeles, California.

Project MKULTRA, or MK-ULTRA, was the code name for a CIA mind-control research program that began in 1950, run by the Office of Scientific Intelligence, and following the release, in that same year, of Ron Hubbard's 'Dianetics: The Modern Science of Mental Health', resuming his unique findings in the field of Mental Health, and which where revolutionary for the time.

There is much published evidence suggesting that MK-Ultra involved the use of many types of drugs to manipulate individual mental states and to alter brain function, and so, it was indeed in the interests of the CIA to have control over Scientology for these experiments.

The possibility of L. Ron Hubbard being murdered by the CIA, in order to divert Scientology for the purposes of the Secret Services, and MK-Ultra in particular, and with the cooperation of David Miscavige — or maybe by Miscavige himself — was reinforced again in 2019, by Guy White — Hubbard's son-in-law.

In an exclusive interview to the Daily Mail TV, he mentioned accessing the coroner report related to the death of Ron Hubbard, and reading that the founder was injected with several psychotic drugs.

He also found that the will of Hubbard had been changed in the exact day before he died. And that this will moved the majority of the money from the family of Ron Hubbard to the Religious Technology Center of David Miscavige.

Guy White also said that his family didn't even know that Ron Hubbard was hill, and that, following the death of the founder, David Miscavige launched a campaign determined at removing all the family members of Ron Hubbard from the Church.

Then, he said, the name of Ron Hubbard had disappeared from many documents, and by 1989 Scientology was a completely different religion.

Many of the former members of the Church of Scientology have publicly stated in their websites that, "Since the death of the founder of the Movement, the Church of Scientology has completely strayed from the original philosophy and purpose of the group which Hubbard first researched and developed" (In Freezone Scientology).

This said, it all points in the direction of a plot to murder the founder of Scientology, and then move the Church to the hands of the CIA under the leadership of David Miscavige.

Nevertheless, since then, many Scientologists have been blindly worshipping and following their own greatest enemy.

THE ANTICHRIST: THE GRAND PLAN OF TOTAL GLOBAL ENSLAVEMENT

Despite the fact that Scientologists believe they oppose Psychiatry, it is certain that David Miscavige is helping studies in Psychiatry for the past decades and through the CIA, and that the reports made about members of Scientology fit into that agenda.

Many Scientologists are very likely CIA agents themselves.

Chapter 58: Who Murdered the Founder of Scientology?

According to a report in the New York Times (1986), "The death of L. Ron Hubbard, the founder of the Church of Scientology, was announced by officials of the organization... County officials said that Mr. Hubbard was cremated without an autopsy".

Ron Hubbard had not been seen in public during the six years prior to his death, and "According to his death certificate, which was signed by Dr. Eugene Denk, a Scientologist who had been Mr. Hubbard's personal physician for many years, he died of a stroke".

George S. Whiting, the county coroner, said in an interview, that he regretted that he was "Forbidden from ordering an autopsy by a certificate of religious preference, purportedly signed by Mr. Hubbard, declaring his objection to an autopsy" (In the New York Times).

This was, most likely, another of the many signature forgeries presented by David Miscavige. But Hubbard's ashes were then "Scattered at sea," according to a spokesman for the Scientology Organization, and "Several former Church officials alleged that Mr. Hubbard had directed them to secretly divert more than $100 million from Church coffers into foreign bank accounts" (In the New York Times).

Again, David Miscavige, as we already know, and has been proven, did that himself, using falsified signatures. The founder was never present.

In an open letter, directed by the former members of Scientology, also known as Free Scientologists (2007), Andreas Groz exposed David Miscavige as a CIA source.

In this letter, he says:

"The Hubbard family was pushed onto the sidelines, the Church of Scientology was taken over by its enemy, Certificates were practically cancelled, only a few regained them, and new Auditors are hardly made. The Church of Scientology was made into a cult: Belief placed over knowledge, obedience over communication, methods of intimidation prevail,... Ethics and PTS-Tech (anticrime techniques) are misused to persecute Field auditors as Squirrels, to disqualify responsible Scientologists as being critical and to exclude Big Beings and opinion leaders in Scientology as suppressive persons... All the key positions are occupied by the big players of the Intelligence Community: MI6, CIA, Mossad. But the take over plan is not any more just the suppression of Scientology. The International Intelligence Community is interested in the psy-tech, the possibility for remote-viewing, to look into the enemies secrets, the possibility to influence people telepathically,... They want to join in."

These Secret Agencies were strongly interested in the many secrets of Ron Hubbard and, quite obviously, found a way to assassinate him. If Miscavige did it with his own hands, or simply observed it happening, is irrelevant! What matters here is that Miscavige is a traitor and a criminal in the leadership of Scientology.

The fact that Miscavige and Tom Cruise are great friends, shows you that this actor is not a very bright individual, neither are those who join Miscavige in anything he does.

However, Miscavige did a grave mistake in the process, that may very well cause his downfall: He stupidly eliminated the copyrights of the founder.

Chapter 59: What Scientologists Don't Want You to Know.

In general, people do get better with the application of the research results presented by Ron Hubbard, and such information is publicly available, as the Church of Spiritual Technology of David Miscavige, founded in 1982, is only in possession of the copyrights of their own alterations to the originals.

These originals went into public domain with the cancellation of the Hubbard Association of Scientologists International, per US law.

According to the True Source Scientology Foundation, "Founded to defend the right to religious freedom of all Scientologists, independently of whether they are a member of the Church of Scientology or not,... What was done by the CST - Church of Spiritual Technology and their associates, during the 80s and 90s is very strange – they copyrighted a lot of materials under 'L.Ron Hubbard Library', all of which were alterations of originals, which in fact means that just the altered portions of the texts and books are protected by copyright, not the originals.

These were more than 4,000 copyright notices handed in to the Library of Congress. So the question is, why would they do so? And the formal explanation given by the CST 'doing business as L.Ron Hubbard Library' is strongly indicating that the original copyrights were lost for some reason or other."

The copyright note on the original work of L. Ron Hubbard says that, "All copyrights, marks and rights, are the property and will remain the property of HCO", meaning that the HCO does not allow any right to further transfer it to any other person. Which would also mean that any assignment done by CSC is invalid. And with its dissolution, the copyrights have fallen into the public domain.

In the website of Scientology, in regard to the copyrights of the Church, it is said that, "While L. Ron Hubbard's lectures had been previously assembled from around the world and stored in archives, the poor quality of the original recordings and deterioration of master tapes seriously impaired mass reproduction. To reclaim Mr. Hubbard's lectures, the Church established one of the world's most sophisticated sound restoration studios.

Mr. Miscavige was intimately involved with every aspect of this project. He dedicated thousands of hours to ensure that every word conformed precisely to Mr. Hubbard's original works and that his recorded lectures were universally accessible. For only in this way can Scientologists chronologically study their religion in pure, unadulterated form."

Indeed, it is interesting how the words are played here with different meanings, as:

- "Reclaim", means they lost the copyrights;

- "Mr. Miscavige was intimately involved", because he had to make sure the originals were altered enough to be protected by copyright law;

- "Only in this way can Scientologists chronologically study their religion in pure, unadulterated form", is indeed true, considering that the Scientologists' Religion is not the original Church of Scientology anymore. Notice that the word Scientology is not applied here but rather "their religion", because 'their religion' is David Miscavige's RTC — Religious Technology Center.

As Wikipedia.org indicates: "The Religious Technology Center (RTC) is an American non-profit corporation that was founded in 1982 by the Church of Scientology to control and oversee the use of all of the trademarks, symbols and texts of Scientology and Dianetics." In other words, RTC is a "non-profit Corporation", not a Religion, founded to "control and oversee the use of all of the trademarks, symbols and texts".

Scientologists' Religion is, in fact, a Corporation, and not the original Church of Scientology.

THE ANTICHRIST: THE GRAND PLAN OF TOTAL GLOBAL ENSLAVEMENT

When someone pays for a course, it is indicated in the receipt that it was a "donation" because, otherwise, the payment would be seen as illegal to a "non-profit". And it is not a non-profit but a scam!

When Scientologists are told that their Organization should pay taxes, they often respond with vicious words and insults, because they were brainwashed to protect their own scammers.

The free copyright of the materials of Scientology includes the right to have access to the original, unaltered works of L.Ron Hubbard. According to the Free Scientologists Organization, "The legal gag, with which CST/RTC try to threaten and handle the Churches and Scientologists, are like the shadows in catching fish on the lake of Tanganjika. Every single Church can easily shake off RTC and CST. Their control is only a shadow, not real power!"

Seven years delivery of auditing and training (without RTC licenses) by the Free Scientologists happened in several countries in the open, without any lawsuits or attacks by RTC — Religious Technology Center. And so, what they can do, others can do also!

Single Field Auditors as well as whole Organizations — staffs and executives — just have to setup a new registered organization, without subjugation under RTC and the mother church (as this did not exist in Ron's days). In fact, the first organizations of Scientology during Ron Hubbard's period were free and independent.

Basically, anyone can continue to use the materials of L. Ron Hubbard or buy new old ones on eBay. Even if the old materials don't shine as pretty as the new, they are original and written by the founder, and not altered by anyone else, and only that counts under the law and to provide techniques which are aligned with the purpose of the founder and not the guidelines of David Miscavige.

David Miscavige owns the copyrights of the altered editions of the works of L. Ron Hubbard. He does not own the copyrights of the original works!

Any threats made by the Church of Scientology on those who published the original works or altered versions of such works, will never be backed by the law! In essence, there is no such thing as the Church of Scientology anymore. The Church of David Miscavige — The Church of Spiritual Technology, is the organization that now represents Scientology.

In essence, what Scientologists don't want you to know, is that you can own Scientology too, by taking possession over the materials as Miscavige did. This is the loophole in Scientology that allows to end it as a Corporation under the authority of one single man.

Chapter 60: The Question Scientologists Never Answer!

We should ask ourselves: What is Scientology without the original materials of the founder? And why is the logo of the Church of David Miscavige similar to the eyes of a snake?

David Miscavige, by cooperating with the CIA, and with the help of several lawyers, falsified signatures and managed to steal the whole Church to his own leadership, but he didn't manage to own the copyrights of the materials in his possession. He mistakenly set them into the public domain. Even though he managed to create his own Corporation by stealing the Organization of Hubbard.

In the Wikipedia page of David Miscavige, it says that he is "The leader of the Church of Scientology", but also says that "His official title is Chairman of the Board of the Religious Technology Center (RTC), a Corporation that controls the trademarks and copyrights of Dianetics and Scientology". So, yes, he controls the trademarks and copyrights, but of the altered materials only. He is the chairman of his own Corporation, because the RTC belongs to him.

The most well-kept secret in Scientology, then appears to be that their materials are all copyright free. Because, just imagine someone publishing all the books online and recordings of the founder! The Religious Technology Center of David Miscavige would end!

That is why they put so many efforts in packaging the materials with nice printing covers, and in selling entire bundles and collections, and creating huge courses that include different books, and which they previously chopped into smaller ones, to make more money, instead of selling individual works separated from the rest.

This also explains why, whenever I asked the Church of Scientology for permission to research and use their technology as part of my own work, the result was always a complete silence — I was not criticized, stopped or allowed.

Because answering me would lead to the revealing of this secret: That the Church of Scientology is the Church of David Miscavige, and he owns the rights to his own adaptations only. Nothing else!

Miscavige eventually created what is called the New Golden Era, claiming to the Scientologists of the time that he found evidence of mistakes in the original works of the founder, to hide the fact that the truth is that the originals are copyright free, and he had to change them in order to regain copyrights over the books and justify such changes. And, because all Scientologists had studied the originals, and not the faked altered versions, the only way to convince them that the new editions were the real thing, was by making them re-read, and restart from the beginning, in his own spiritual bridge.

Scientologists not only restarted their studies but also had to pay for everything again.

Talking about a double scam! This makes David Miscavige the master of all scams!

Just imagine some University calling their students and saying: "I am sorry but your college degree and diploma are not valid anymore. Because we found that most of your teachers were based on incorrect information. We had to make several corrections and changes to those books. Therefore, you have to come back and do it all over again, as your diploma isn't valid any longer... Ah yes, you'll also have to pay for it, again. Full price! No discounts possible! That is, if you wish to keep the position you have right now, or your job, and that you acquired after a lifetime of studies and struggles. Which are all, starting from now, invalid!"

People don't seem to be able to separate the books from the Church, because it is obvious there's nothing wrong with the works of the founder but with the Organization claiming to represent Scientology, under David Miscavige. But this is a story that works as an example that applies as well to the many other groups. For the Vatican did the same with the gnostic scrolls. You can compare

THE ANTICHRIST: THE GRAND PLAN OF TOTAL GLOBAL ENSLAVEMENT

the original Bible with the modern one, and see that, what different religions are offering people, no matter their name or how they promote themselves, is very distinct from what the first Christians were teaching.

The Bible is a brainwashing manual. The original writings — The gnostic texts — are very and much more profound in meaning. But that, you don't get!

In fact, the different religious branches of Christianity, to claim a lineage from the real Christianity, should be including all the gnostic texts inside their Bible. And yet, they refuse to do that! No matter how many branches there are for Christians to choose from, they all follow the same fake bible!

Can you learn from a fake bible? Sure, as much as the Scientologists of today can learn from the fake works of L. Ron Hubbard. But when a book is edited or mistranslated, much is lost. And only those who are smart enough to compare the information, or know the truth, will ever see it.

The gap can be so vast, that it will seem like the original knowledge was significantly downgraded. Just as much as when you try to compare an orange juice made out of squeezed oranges with a package containing mostly water with color and sugars.

Most religions today are nothing more than artificial constructions of downgraded works, to keep the masses stupid and in the dark.

Chapter 61: The Illusion of Salvation.

As the spiritual suffering increases in the world, some people turn to religion for forgiveness and salvation, while others sink into a state of self-abasement, in which they deliberately deteriorate everything around them, namely, their relationships, with their spouse and children, they friends, and even their appearance and attitude to life.

Being a total disgrace has become so normalized, most don't try to fight back. Being a whore was once something to be ashamed of, and is now a reason for pride. The same applies with being evil and hurting others. Most people actually think, and especially the newest generations, that lack of respect is a sign of social superiority, as if not needing to respect others was a demonstration of strength. And so, many lose themselves in their own lies. Anyway. it is now easy to forget someone and erase that person from our life, with a click of a button that says "block".

This narcissistic view of life also causes that many want to impose their own limitations on others, when saying things like, "That's not how you survive in the real world", "You should shut up", "We all accept it and you should as well", and "Only insane people do that".

When the outer reality doesn't match the inner reality, a button, implanted by the same social programming, activates, and gives a clear organic emotion of danger to its host, in which lack of logic leads to the feeling of imminent destruction and the sense of confusion at the same time.

This is why people tend to lack the ability to deal with new information, especially if it contradicts and threatens their own understandings of reality.

Education does such a good job in indoctrinating people, that even the most successful believe that they can't do something unless they memorize it and get a degree first.

People don't know that they can study on their own, research on their own, think and analyze by themselves anything they want, and even find meanings for what they can't comprehend in a dictionary. Because they have been programmed to disbelieve their own efforts and natural resources as human learners. They don't trust themselves!

An entire life inside classrooms erases the potential for awareness and self-development. And that's why the vast majority thinks that they need a job to survive. They were manipulated to believe this. And they won't trust anyone who doesn't have a job or, at least, owns an office. They are so immersed in their own movie of what reality is, than anything outside of it, scares them.

Among this vast amount of industrialized slaves, the most successful are doomed to a life of appearances, lies and delusions, with which they are confronted in lonely depressions and slight acknowledgements of a mass schizophrenia, and which they quickly try to reduce by imposing verbal abuse and evil acts on those below them.

That's why arrogance is not only common, but needed as well, among Physicians, Psychiatrists, College Professors, Engineers, etc. Arrogance is the ultimate defense of the ego, when the ego is afraid of becoming conscious of itself.

Madness and despair are the fears that arrogant individuals truly hide, to suppress their disbelief in what they do in life and life itself. They can't be awaken but only share their own suffering with others.

Chapter 62: Thinking Positive and Being Unconscious.

The idea that one can be a positive thinker without being awaken, has become popularized among the fools, that can't handle the contradiction within themselves.

The higher someone is in the social hierarchy, the stronger are his attachments to a social identity, body and belongings. Reason why politicians are so easily corrupted. Dependency on a social image, hides the panic of being threatened by the light of truth. And yet, when the fear of the truth consumes the soul, there's no resistance anymore to the interference of demons. And that's why countless exorcists have been warning us on the rapidly increasing number of possessed souls.

Most people believe they are smart and forget who is thinking for them when they are not producing their own thoughts. Within their ego, they are oblivious to spiritual influences.

They are simply not aware — they lack spiritual awareness.

Demonically implanted fears then tell them...

- "You are what you see and what you have;
- If what you see and have isn't real, you are not real;
- If your possessions have no value, you have no value."

Due to such inner beliefs, people then tell themselves, when facing contradictions between reality and the truth: "I am real! I am real!".

That's why, when people face more problems, they run faster and they work harder, just like an hamster inside a wheel. That wheel is all they know and all they can see. But they are worse than the hamster, because the hamster doesn't have consciousness or a sense of self-worth or social-worth. People, on the other hand, increase both with what they have, and so, they always have a reason to work harder and make more money.

This problem is so serious, that when you meet someone, the first questions, wherever you are in the entire world, are always the same:

- "What do you for a living?"
- "Where are you from?".
- "Why are you here?"

The questions are always the same because the program operating in the background of their mind is always the same. It is as if you were dealing with the same robots, coming from the same manufacturer.

They are predictable because they are unconscious to their predictability. They are unconscious of their mental state! They are unaware that they are spiritually dead.

These questions also and immediately filter you and simultaneously judge your value within the same social paradigms. The answer is then quantified and qualified based on personal assumptions.

Never does the one who asks these limiting questions assumes his own limitations.

Whenever I answered to anyone, "I do what I want with my time", "It doesn't matter where I am from, or "I am here because I want," I raised suspicions, and created fear and avoidance, as if I was committing a crime in the world.

Often, that is exactly what people assume about me, that I am a criminal. Most accused me of selling drugs or being a possible hitman, because they can't believe anything I say or do, even if I spend entire days in front of my computer.

THE ANTICHRIST: THE GRAND PLAN OF TOTAL GLOBAL ENSLAVEMENT

Many of the women who lived with me, actually thought I was a spy, and couldn't believe I write books, even when seeing me do it in front of their eyes. This reality is simply not seen! And because I am not a credible human being, it is as if I was a ghost in the eyes of many. They cannot process my existence!

Some of the people I met actually confessed that they avoided me, because they never met anyone like me, and that scared them. Even if nothing I said or did to them could justify that fear. It was simply the fear of the unknown.

People avoid the unknown! They rather trust a lie than try to understand a truth!

Social life has became so dependent on social worth, that friendships, kindness and happiness, in themselves, have suddenly became obsolete. Everything needs to be quantified and justified based on social validation, even if people are unaware that the social norms and values are being manipulated. They don't care, and the more they drift away from this fact, the less they want to think about it.

The efforts are too many for their mind to process! It would collapse their entire system of beliefs, and nullify the value of their existence. They rather be an imaginary being than a real but lost one.

The personality of many is therefore fake, because that is all they know. Their arrogance becomes a desperate need to protect this mask. For they don't know who they are without it.

Chapter 63: Why Love Became a Rare Commodity?

Most people are stuck in a very basic level of survival rooted on instinct. As a result, they behave according to what the social system tells them to do — which is, fundamentally, to compete and become better than others.

That's why the majority lives within a paradigm of fight or flight. Which means they'll abandon anyone or anything that doesn't match their reality and identity, and will fight to destroy what threatens that same reality and identity.

Once people are deeply immersed in the system that supports them, they will protect it with their life. And this means, in this case, to have one's identity attached to this same system. And so, love is, for the vast majority, merely a means by which they satisfy narcissist desires, working in their favor when helping them keep others, or to destroy them along the way.

Suddenly, in a highly materialistic driven world, love became both a tool of punishment and reward, that most offer when receiving something in return, and take from those they wish to punish. Reason why, nowadays, books entitled "How to make someone love you", are far more popular than books entitled "How to love someone". But even the most religious, when talking about love, tend to contradict themselves within this same fear, and believe that love must be earned. They don't know that it is just a quality that you awaken within yourself, with or without religion, or even spirituality; and that you can benefit when loving someone.

Scientists have proven countless times that, "When we are falling in love, chemicals associated with the reward circuit flood our brain, producing a variety of physical and emotional responses" (Richard Schwartz and Jacqueline Olds, In Harvard Medical School).

A study conducted at Stony Brook University in New York (2011), also found that it is possible to be madly in love with someone after decades of marriage. The research team performed MRI scans on couples who had been married an average of 21 years, and found the same intensity of activity in dopamine-rich areas of the brains as found in the brains of couples who were newly in love.

This study suggested that the excitement of romance can remain while the apprehension is lost. This investigation of love has confirmed for the very first time that people are not lying when they say that after 10 to 30 years of marriage they are still madly in love with their partners.

Other studies have proven that empathy in itself, even towards strangers, improves our overall health. In 1990, Heather Marie Higgins, PhD, conducted a study to look at the effects of empathy training on the stress medical students are under in emotional circumstances. What Dr. Higgins found was that, those who undergo empathy training interacted with patients with more compassion, yet their stress levels in emotionally intense encounters decreased.

It's a counterintuitive finding because most people assume that empathy is the ability to "walk in other people's shoes" as it were. So when you empathize with someone in a negative state, the logic follows, you'd increase your stress instead of decreasing it. But the opposite is actually true. Those who lack the ability to empathize often pick up the stress of others without knowing why. The researchers found that stress spread just as quickly as common cold does.

One of the reasons pointed for this phenomenon was the so called 'mirror neurons' – special brain cells that allow us to mimic what others are feeling, subconsciously. And because empathy involves understanding what others are going through (which is a conscious activity), those who do it well are resistant to the negative influence of second-hand stress, and therefore saving themselves from all its health implications.

Now, if research after research, continue on showing us the importance of love, as in empathy and compassion, or even romance, why are people more and more isolated and suspicious or apathetic towards each other? Why has love become a rare commodity?

Chapter 64: Why People Don't Want to Show Compassion?

The media pushes a counterintuitive narrative to enforce certain beliefs in the masses, such as: "Look! If you feel, is love". And then, we share in social networks something like: "Love! Feel Love! Go and find that feeling!". And, as a result, most people get hurt in this type of decadent love, because it is based on conquering, obtaining, stealing, taking, as if being a fake and manipulative person was the only way of obtaining love, and love was something that we take, an emotion, that we harvest from someone else.

The media also offers answers to such outcome, as if it possessed the whole truth. It says: "Love hurts but it's worth the pain". And so, people go again into the same path, and end up spending an entire lifetime inside the cycle of 'survive and destroy'.

Most people are so inside this mental program, that they end up marrying exactly the one who makes them feel worse, as they believe that love is all about suffering.

Wanting the one that hurts or adds value to our social status is the most common implant for human love. Only a very small amount of people in this world have realized that they are not what they see but what they feel.

Such people don't seek love outside themselves but rather feel it as part of a whole and observe it in anything that inspires harmony and transmits balance, from a flower to a painting, or even old and young people they meet and the empathic connections they build around themselves.

These very few individuals have an identity that they have found beyond their brain and their body. And they know that they can't explain it, because nobody told them the words that allow expressing such inner world. The social system in which they where born doesn't consider them on purpose.

These type of individuals, may feel depressed and sad about the world they live in, because they can't identify the same type of compassion in others, in the vast majority. But they can also feel a special type of happiness and peace inside their own world. For such individuals tend to either be creative or obtain their happiness from nature, or both — art and nature.

Such people have a very different approach from the rest of mankind, that is running away from their own truth and can only find peace and happiness inside a group of people sharing the same lunatic ideas about reality; people that often have many friends, because they're not awaked to their true self. And yet, when these friends are all together, they seem more like a bunch of autistic individuals talking alone. Nobody truly cares about anyone in the group.

If they were awake, they would see how lonely they are in this insane world, and would refuse any type of illusion, even if it meant to be seen as a lunatic or outcast by others. And yet, most are so afraid to lose these illusions, that they go back to them and push away those who can awaken them.

It is not difficult to identify the chosen ones that the Bible talks about, because people who truly feel empathy are so extremely rare, you may not even find it in a religious congregation.

Chapter 65: Are Modern Christians Capable of Loving Others?

In 1970, a research was conducted by the Princeton University, in which seminary students were sent on urgent assignments designed to take them past an actor posing as a person in need of assistance. Researchers measured whether (and how) students interrupted their pressing tasks to render help, and analyzed the results.

The actor portraying a homeless man was Jeremiah Steepek — the new head pastor of a very large church. After spending half an hour incognito in his new church prior to services and finding that only a very few congregants would even return his greeting (much less respond to his pleas for money to buy food), he reveals himself to his new flock and delivers to them a lesson in Christian compassion.

In June 2013, the Rev. Willie Lyle — the newly-appointed pastor of the Sango United Methodist Church in Clarksville, Tennessee — conducted a similar research, and spent four and a half days living in the streets in the guise of a homeless man. He then transformed back into his role as pastor as he delivered a sermon, saying the following:

"In a dream, God told Willie that he needed to live on the streets of Clarksville as a homeless and hungry person. He challenged Willie to experience firsthand just what it was like to have nothing — no home, no money, no friends, no food on even a semi-regular basis, no nothing... In those four and a half days, he learned a great deal about the homeless, the working poor who face hunger daily and those in need of spiritual and emotional help. It was not comfortable... He wondered how many people would approach him and offer him food, or a place to sit inside an air conditioned room, or just see how they could help. Twenty people spoke to him and offered some type of assistance..."

He was speaking to 200 people who gathered that morning, meaning that 90% of them did not offer any help or compassion towards that homeless man.

This is why Pastor Lyle told them: "Often the least used parts of the body are the ones that mean the most, like our heart and mind... Too many of us only want to serve God one hour each week. That doesn't cut it. That is not God's plan."

Months later, in November 2013, Mormon Bishop David Musselman posed as a homeless man and interacted with congregants outside a Taylorsville, Utah, church before services one Sunday. At least five people asked David Musselman to leave the church property in Taylorsville, some gave him money and most were indifferent.

Musselman then said to them upon revealing himself:

"Many actually went out of their way to purposefully ignore me, and they wouldn't even make eye contact,... I'd approach them and say, 'Happy Thanksgiving.' Many of them I wouldn't ask for any food or any kind of money, and their inability to even acknowledge me being there was very surprising."

What do all these studies show us?

Well, they show us that, on average, about 90% of the Christians are fake. They do not have any compassion, they show no empathy, and they do no represent the founder of their movement — Jesus Christ — or the religions they preach.

God, quite clearly, is not with them!

Could this result be extended to other religions? Most certainly!

More than 90% of the Freemasons, Rosicrucians, Buddhists, Hindus, among many others, as I have seen for myself, do not represent their own founders or even books and beliefs. I have caught many of the leaders of these groups I mentioned contradicting their own books as well.

Many of them have actually insulted me out of jealousy, as it was confirmed by some who have already died from old age.

As in the times of Jesus Christ, the world is full of hypocrites!

THE ANTICHRIST: THE GRAND PLAN OF TOTAL GLOBAL ENSLAVEMENT

Therefore, do not fool yourself by the fact that there are many Christians in the world. For they are just numbers, not representatives of their faith!

Chapter 66: The Chosen Ones.

What makes the chosen ones so different from the rest — the vast majority? And how to identify them?

A study conducted by Rita Meneses, from The University of Birmingham, on empathy, showed that, people who have more empathy, and thus put more emphasis in their communication, by sharing personal experiences, insights and emotions, tend to build more meaningful relationships with others.

According to her study, "Verbal communication, in itself, was not as meaningful as when it was associated with a significant way of knowing (intuiting, sharing, imagining). That is, communication for the sake of communication was important for the conversation to evolve in a pleasant continuous manner, but it did not transform that moment into a significant one, it did not transform the verbal comment into a significant one... [However] discussing shared experiences had a beneficial impact upon the relationship (in this context) and intensified the sharing experience itself... Viewing sometimes made participants realize that they were having a shared experience, and non-verbally manifesting it... The nonverbal dimension of the communication mattered little for imaginative experiences to come about and be meaningful".

Those who have no empathy are truly very poor in spirit, for this study shows us as well that we are inside of ourselves as we are outside. We can only build relationships that empower us and elevate us spirituality, if we are willing to open ourselves to others and share our own experience — by communicating with our emotions, insights, intuition and overall perceptions.

In this sense, once you change your attitude towards the outside, so will your vibration change, and along with it, the perceptions others make of you.

In this process, to see our friends abandon us, as we change our vibration and tune to a new and higher frequency, is a blessing. As those who haven't abandoned us, are covertly, in their own perception of love, often trying to change us back into who we were.

On the other hand, to a detachment from others is also a sign of holding on to attachments, because in the spiritual realm of our universe, there's no time, space or distance — We are and will always be connected to those we can see and hold in our mind and heart, either they are alive or dead, as the spirit lives forever and connections exist in the same frequency wherever we are. The real world has no time or space, and in this world consciousness can be instantaneous.

This mindset allows us to connect to life at a very different level — emotional, visual and even telepathic. For we are as God in our full potential as humans — peaceful, creative, self-sufficient and naturally joyful.

Only illusions can trap us inside the feelings of loss, anxiety and distress. But the whole world is an illusion made to blind us from the truth. And why should we try to keep those who will permanently reject us, as we move forward in life? They are not at the same frequency. They can't handle a different vibration towards existence. And, if you give them a chance, they will do their best to turn you into one of them, because that's the only thing they can do — replicate.

The path of truth is a lonely journey, but a very fulfilling one, where we can always find someone to hold our soul when we feel tired. Most of the times, they will come out of nowhere, when we least expect but need them the most.

A true life, and a life of truth, is a life full of amazing and positive surprises, and a constant development towards the enlightenment or consciousness. And it is also a life of detachments, that often uncover the best spiritual discoveries within ourselves.

In such a state of being, we allow our personality to die, in order to reincarnate with a new awareness, and reborn again with a new goal for our future. We then understand the process of resurrection from a very different perspective — fundamentally, pragmatic and fulfilling.

Chapter 67: The Choice that is Asked!

One way or another, we all have the option to choose in which reality we want to live while creating our future. But the acceptance of the reality that is given to us, implies an acceptance of the World Order of the Power Elite, and namely, their religious plans:

- One Religion for the masses — An atheistic religion, based on promiscuity, lack of love, the rejection of the soul, the values of science and the worshipping of the government as the highest state of awareness;

- One religion for the elite — An integration of ancient religions into one body of knowledge, namely, paganism, judaism, and demonology, while using science in the pursuit of a higher spirituality, through the access to past lives and the development of the mind. As such, the masses will embrace transhumanism, by becoming as cyborgs — mind controlled slaves —, while the Elites merges with the AI to gain immortality.

The type of government expected is, nonetheless, the same for both groups: A Technocratic Dictatorship mixing the principles of democracy and communism in one body of values.

The police force would be a United Nations Military Force. And the banking system is for sure expected to be controlled by the Rothschild Dynasty, through the centralization of the Bank of England, the Federal Reserve and the Bank of the Vatican.

Medicine in this New World would, again, as with religion, be divided between:

- The medicine of the people — A Rockefeller Controlled Program, blending psychiatry, mandatory and periodic vaccination, and pharmaceutical drugs;

- And the medicine of the Elite — holistic, natural and based on the highest scientific advances known to mankind — most likely, using alien technology as well.

This world will not appear in one day. We have been heading towards it for a very long time, and more precisely, for the past one hundred years. As such, people will assume, as now, that it is their decision to go that way, as they always did.

The idea that the masses control their own reality and history is random have been the two of the biggest lies ever told.

We are, however, still on time to reverse these outcomes and change the future of mankind. For as long as there are writers to write about the truth, and readers to trust this truth, we can sill have hope.

On the other hand, people have to be motivated to search for the truth. Most aren't!

Obviously, if the majority of the people have narcissistic tendencies, and show no compassion towards strangers, it is only predictable that, from this mass of imbeciles, psychopaths — those who, despite not having any empathy, possess a tremendous greed for power and control — can obtain positions of influence in society and reach the top of the social hierarchy. After all, if empathy and love aren't valued, then social value will have to come through ruthless power and fear, even if abused.

As multibillionaire Dan Peña have said several times, including in a seminar recorded in 2019, "Fear doesn't get the job done, but fear works, and fear with beatings (pain) works best".

The main point is that, if "Love doesn't get the job done", as Dan Peña says, then you have to get value and respect with the opposite perspective, which is the same as to say that power and wealth can only be obtained through the ways that those who lack empathy understand, and that's control through fear and pain.

THE ANTICHRIST: THE GRAND PLAN OF TOTAL GLOBAL ENSLAVEMENT

That is precisely why salaries are never above a certain national level, related to the overall cost of living, and diseases are used against the people to control them.

The two things, disease and scarcity, keep billions of people under control. And could it be done in any other way?

Many who defend the application of the 'universal basic income' think that the world can truly function with a bunch of lazy people without any empathy for each other. And yet, the Elite disagrees, or they wouldn't put so many efforts to vaccinate and chip everyone as if they were mere cattle. For the only moment in time, when such thing as a basic income is given, is when everyone receiving it has been microchiped and is being monitored 24 hours a day with surveillance cameras.

In fact, this has been explained by Dan Peña himself, when addressing the power of fear. Peña often uses the example of his own father to explain how fear works. He says that, when his father was questioned and condemned for his actions, by his brother and sister, he used to say to them: "How is your program working on your slut daughter you got? And what about the heroin asshole son you got, that is in the penitentiary, how is your program working with your boy?"

His story proves to be true to a larger scale. Countless studies have shown that single motherhood ruins children's lives, as single mothers cause disproportionately high crime rates, mental health issues, drug abuse and education problems.

The same studies show that single fathers do not have such a negative impact. It's the mothers that become destructive when not supervised by men. As the studies reveal,...

- 43% of prison inmates, grew up in a single-parent household — 39% with their mothers, and 4% with their fathers (In US Bureau of Justice Statistics);

- 60% of rapists and 72% of murderers grew up without fathers (In Behavioral Sciences and the Law, Life Without a Father, Policy Review);

- 63% of suicides are from fatherless homes (In US Department of Health Census);

- 85% of all children who show behavioral disorders come from fatherless homes, according to the Center for Disease Control;

- 71% of all high school dropouts come from fatherless homes, according to the National Principals Association Report;

- 75% of all adolescent patients in chemical abuse centers come from fatherless homes.

What this tells us is basically that, as the vast majority of society is gradually becoming less empathic, more violent and more selfish, only enslavement and control through absolute terror can work.

This is what people asked for, when embracing values that destroy families, create distrust in society and deny the importance of love, marriage, family and God.

Promiscuity, selfishness, and materialism, but mostly, lack of compassion and lack of empathy, have destroyed the entire world.

In such a world, only psychopaths would know how to rule with efficiency. And this is why the majority of the morons in the entire planet keep praising and worshiping the psychopaths at the top, represented right now by Bill Gates, George Soros, Hillary Clinton and many others associated with them, through the Rockefeller Foundation or the Rothschild Banking System.

Chapter 68: The Leaders of The New World Order.

The leaders of the New World Order will certainly be very cruel and evil. And it is not difficult to analyze how they will think, as many of the current leaders show a similar predisposition.

Psychopaths think in a similar way. Therefore, the leaders of the future, will all have some pleasure in hurting others.

Not all psychopaths are narcissists but all narcissists are psychopaths. And usually, psychopaths who want power, are narcissists. This is obvious in their words and their lack of empathy for human suffering. But nothing is worse than applauding them, as what occurred when Bill Gates said publicly: "If we do a really good job on new vaccines and healthcare, we can lower the world population by 10 to 15%."

People often think that psychopaths who murder are the most dangerous. It's a common mistake. But the most dangerous ones are actually those who make you kill yourself, by accepting a vaccine, or a psychotropic drug or any other form of destroying your health. They operate in a similar manner to those who try to convince someone to commit suicide.

In regards to this last type, I must say that one of the most interesting things people say is: "I can't be manipulated because I always do what I want"; as that is exactly how manipulation occurs; it is always through the idea that you are in control of your own decisions.

Communism, Psychiatry, Hollywood, Religion, and the Educational System, among many other means, have as their main purpose to make people believe that they are in control of their fate. That is precisely why so much money and research is invested in these fields.

Moreover, the belief that mind control isn't occurring because people are free to make their own choices, is the greatest trick ever pulled on mankind.

People are not truly making free choices anymore. They are being persuaded from birth, through many institutions and scientific bodies, by the media, and by society itself, by their own family even, into believing what they are supposed to believe. And their beliefs are not independent. They are withheld within the community beliefs.

Most people take pride in being aligned with the beliefs of the majority, in being trendy and accepted by many. They think this flock thinking pattern makes them right, and by default, they assume that being different and discriminated is wrong. And that's exactly how they are manipulated.

If you are afraid of ridicule and discrimination, not just from society in general, but from your friends and relatives, you are clearly under mind control.

Unless you try to do something that they will oppose, you have never risked going out of your comfort zone. But that isn't difficult to do. All you need is try to start a business of your own. As most of such people certainly have jobs, they will do their best to stop you.

If you think that all of your thoughts belong to you, the same applies. For one needs to question himself and the values of those around him often and always, before he can consider himself free. And yet, once he is free, he will not possess freedom for as long as those around him discriminate him for being free and independent. He merely awakens to the fact that he is in a gigantic bubble-prison with many layers. And he has merely escaped the spiritual layer — not the social, psychological and emotional layers. He would have to be an outcast for that to happen.

Being an outcast — isolated from the rest of the world — is just another form of being in a prison — the prison of social, psychological and emotional loneliness.

As Leslie Wagner-Wilson, former member of the Peoples Temple, led by mass murdered Pastor Jim Jones, said in an interview in 2017: "That happened because we are all looking for a place to fit into the world; we are looking for love, we are looking for acceptance, and Jim Jones provided that."

THE ANTICHRIST: THE GRAND PLAN OF TOTAL GLOBAL ENSLAVEMENT

Leslie lost a total of eleven relatives, including her husband, mother, sister, brother, niece and nephew in Jonestown. Because this need to belong to a group is very powerful in the human psyche, and is precisely the most studied method of mass control as well.

In fact, evidence leads us to believe that, what occurred in Jonestown, was just another CIA experiment, to see how far people go in their blind obedience to a leader and need of belonging to a group — looking for acceptance and love.

Jim Jones used to test his people's faith, by making them consume a drink that later he would jokingly say to contain poison. It was his way of pushing his people to higher levels of commitment. But the CIA saw in this test an excellent opportunity to analyze how far the people would go in their faith. Could they actually kill themselves for what they believe?

"Drinking the Kool-Aid became an expression used to refer to a person who believes in a possibly doomed or dangerous idea because of perceived potential high rewards. It can also be used to refer to accepting an idea or changing a preference due to popularity, peer pressure, or persuasion. In recent years it has evolved further to mean extreme dedication to a cause or purpose, so extreme that one would 'drink the Kool-Aid and die for the cause'" (In Wikipedia).

These experiments allowed forming radical groups with ease and improve on the methods of mass control. According to John Judge, author of 'The Untold Story of the Jonestown Massacre', "The real tragedy of Jonestown is not only that it occurred, but that so few chose to ask themselves why or how, so few sought to find out the facts behind the bizarre tale used to explain away the death of more than 900 people, and that so many will continue to be blind to the grim reality of our Intelligence Agencies".

Chapter 69: The Secret Mind Control Experiments.

Nothing gives the Global Elite more pleasure than seeing a religious leader betraying his own followers and murdering them; or seeing criminals giving interviews on live television; or testing the imbecility of a group, as when following the one who murder their own founder, such as with the case of Scientology. This is the ultimate level of control, because it includes ridicule, mind control and ignorance at the highest level possible.

One of the Directors of the CIA — during a period in which the MK-Ultra Mind Control Project was sill in its early stages, Richard Helms — resumed this mindset well, when saying that, "The real problem is arranging that experience in a way that tells a story, which is just incredible enough to be interesting, but credible enough to be believed".

Adolf Hitler (In 'Mein Kampf'), confirmed, by saying that, "In the big lie there is always a certain force of credibility; because the broad masses, in the primitive simplicity of their minds, more readily fall victims to the big lie than the small lie, since they themselves often tell small lies in little matters but would be ashamed to resort to large-scale falsehoods. It would never come into their heads to fabricate colossal untruths, and they would not believe that others could have the impudence to distort the truth so infamously. Even though the facts which prove this to be so may be brought clearly to their minds, they will still doubt and waver and will continue to think that there may be some other explanation."

Similarly, we notice this practice when the Elite gives the public movies that prepare for events ahead, events previously planned in secrecy, and then presented as fiction, as was with the case of movies about terrorism, movies about global pandemics, or movies about apocalyptical catastrophes in which a majority starves to death or turns into zombies that need to eat human flesh in order to survive. All these movies intend to show events to come, and which are being orchestrated.

Their tactics can be resumed in three ways:

- The positioning of the future in the present, as when movies operate like a brainwashing tool using visualization techniques against the people watching them;

- Positioning the past in the present, as when placing criminals in positions of power or on live television, to suppress the collective subconscious with a lie in front of their eyes;

- The use of key-phrases and key-images, mostly of a religious nature, intending to create a network of thoughts in people's head and that combine as a collective synchronicity favoring a predetermined agenda — the collective subconscious then becomes the collective conscious.

Being agreeable or socially accepted then becomes another stage of this control, as the unfit become segregated by the collectivism — a mass composed by the brainwashed, manipulated and drugged through food toxicity.

Many studies in psychology have shown that humans tend to change their views on reality to comply with the rest of the group. All one needs to do, is give the individual the idea that the group is having the belief that it is intended to impose on the individual, and his belief eventually becomes the group belief, in what is termed "self-fulfilling prophecy or the 'chameleon effect'.

In psychology, "The chameleon effect refers to non-conscious mimicry of the postures, mannerisms, facial expressions, and other behaviors of one's interaction partners, such that one's behavior passively and unintentionally changes to match that of others in one's current social environment" (In Wikipedia).

The key characteristic of the social chameleon, just like their reptilian color-changing counterpart, is an ability to blend seamlessly into any social environment. And so, this collectivism is then aligned, as if people were nothing but sheep, in order for the individual — just like a chameleon — to copy the behaviors and beliefs of his group in order to fit it and adapt.

THE ANTICHRIST: THE GRAND PLAN OF TOTAL GLOBAL ENSLAVEMENT

This is why the fear of making others unhappy is another great trap. For as long you are afraid to make your friends and family unhappy with your decisions, you won't make any decision that moves astray from the group.

This collective mindset allows to control large amounts of people as if they were sheep, although, in this case, they keep each other in the group, without the need for barking dogs.

The police gradually becomes unnecessary, not because there is less crime, but because the masses are too brainwashed to revolt.

Chapter 70: MK-Ultra and The Jonestown Massacre.

The study of collectivism in mind control experiments was always extremely crucial to understand how to manipulate large amounts of people into doing something against their will or even nature. This is why religious collectivism has been so important to study how to master large crowds effectively.

The well-known massacre of Jonestown is one of those situations that provided plenty of information to analyze. For it was part of a MK-Ultra Project. The plan followed the same strategy as others orchestrated by the CIA, which is the use of a scapegoat — Jim Jones — to suppress the suspicion on the public of a possible involvement of the Secret Services, and even though much of the truth did come to the surface — a truth so unbelievable that many still find hard to accept.

The official version is that over nine hundred people committed suicide by order of their pastor — Jim Jones. But the Forensic Investigation conducted by Dr. Leslie Mootoo showed that Jim Jones had been shot on the head and there was no evidence proving that the injury was self-inflicted. A conclusion also made by The Armed Forces Institute of Pathology (AFIP) of the United States.

Moreover, Dr. Mootoo, found fresh needle marks at the back of the left shoulder blades of 80-90% of the victims. Others had been shot or strangled, leading Dr. Mootoo to the conclusion that all but three of the people were murdered by "persons unknown".

Charles Huff — a former member of the US Army Special Forces in Panama and one of the seven Green Berets among the first American troops to arrive on the scene following the massacre— told Freedom Magazine: "We saw many bullet wounds as well as wounds from crossbow bolts."

The bodies were then stripped of identification, including the medical wrist tags visible in many early photos. And the transportation of the bodies to the United States was delayed for long enough to make it difficult for any autopsy to detect the real cause of death. An investigation which could lead to the assumption that the victims were subject to psychotropic drugs commonly used by the CIA for mind control experiments.

Officials in New Jersey also complained that state coroners were excluded, and that the military coroners appointed were illegally performing cremations (In New York Times).

In resume, an experiment on a large group of people had been carefully conducted and hidden by the CIA. And the only person who could uncover the whole truth — Jim Jones — was shot dead at the scene. Or was he?

According to Jim Keith, author of "Secret and Suppressed", Jim Jones had and used doubles, which is very unusual for a religious leader, but common in the Secret Services. Photos of his dead body do not show identifying tattoos on his chest, the body and face were not clearly recognizable due to bloating and discoloration, and no dental records check was made.

This massacre followed an attempt of Senator Leo Ryan to uncover the CIA experiment with a team of reporters, and which led him to his own death. Witnesses described the group that shot Senator Leo Ryan to the New York Times, as acting like "zombies," walking mechanically, without any emotion. Most likely, were mercenaries of the CIA, as everyone in that community was part of an experiment — some as victims, and others as well-trained killers.

The targets had been purposefully selected, as only certain people were killed, and the selection was clearly planned. The killers made sure that Ryan and the newsmen were dead, in some cases, by shooting the wounded in the head.

In a desperate attempt to test their conditioning methods, the leaders in the religious group — mostly composed by individuals with connections to the Military or Intelligence Agencies — tried to implement a real suicide drill, leading to a revolt where the majority of the people fled, unaware that there were others waiting to catch them.

THE ANTICHRIST: THE GRAND PLAN OF TOTAL GLOBAL ENSLAVEMENT

The persecution of the survivors continued after the day of the massacre. Jeannie and Al Mills, who intended to write a book about Jim Jones, were murdered at home. The police described the killings as being professional — using dum-dum bullets, leaving no traceable clues, and no signs of forced entry or burglary.

Shortly later on, the Guyanese Ambassador to the United States, Laurence Mann, and his young wife Paula, a survivor from Jonestown, were as well found murdered, along with their infant child. Relatives who had seen him just the night before, said "nothing was wrong".

Also murdered were two politicians — Mayor Moscone and Harvey Milk.

Interesting, is also the fact that the murder of dissents from the Peoples Temple was common even before the massacre. Seven mysterious deaths of members were mentioned by journalist Kathy Hunter of the Ukiah press. These were members who had argued with Jones and attempted to leave his Church.

Jones openly hinted to other members that he had arranged for them to die, while threatening a similar fate to those who would be disloyal (In the New York Times, 1978).

Infractions of the rules or disloyalty often led to forced drugging, physical torture and even public sexual rape and humiliation. Beatings and verbal abuse were also commonplace.

These practices were parallel with the need to study techniques of mass control, behavior programming and reduction of violence, following the researches of Dr. José Delgado, Dr. Vernon Mark, Dr. Frank Ervin and Dr. Jolly West.

Dr. José Delgado, pioneer in the research of behavior modification through electrical signals, actually told Congress that he hoped for a future where a technology would control workers in the field and troops at war with electronic remote signals, stating that electrodes implanted in their brains would make them "both happy and productive".

Chapter 71: Mind Control Technology and Radio-Frequency.

Dr. José Delgado — Professor at Yale University — believed that, "Man does not have the right to develop his own mind. This kind of liberal orientation has great appeal, but we must electrically control the brain".

His belief would inspire the use of the Radio Frequency Identification through implantable microchips (RFID) as a means of mass control through electric signals provided by towers carefully located for this purpose — The 5G Networks.

The worldwide distribution of these towers would then facilitate the global obedience to a New World Government.

The use of such towers as military weaponry of mind control to take over the entire planet, followed the experiments of the CIA on The Peoples Temple Agricultural Project — from 1974 to 1978 —, as the members had orders constantly being imposed on them through megaphones installed in different towers, positioned around the community.

However, the first person to conduct experiments on Radio-frequency and behavior modification was actually Lafayette Ronald Hubbard — founder of Scientology —, through his therapeutical methods, which he named as "Auditing Procedures".

Hubbard published his findings for the first time in 1950, in the book "Dianetics" — which was rejected by mainstream Psychiatry but not ignored. The findings published in Dianetics were then studied by Dr. Delgado, who at the time that the book was released, had just accepted a position in the Physiology Department of Yale. Dr. Delgado would publish his studies on implanting electrodes into humans only years later.

Dr. Joye Jeffries Pugh confirmed this (In Eden, 2006) when he said that, "Dr. Delgado's scientific work began in the 1950's, when his mind control tactics were funded by the Naval Intelligence and the Air Force."

The need to steal such information from Scientology and pass it to the CIA, was linked to the experiments developed by Dr. Jose Delgado and the Jonestown experiment, because once Hubbard identified the frequencies of the human body, according to different emotions and thoughts, he made it possible to study the manipulation of such frequencies as well.

According to Hubbard, it was possible to change the thoughts of a person and rehabilitate an individual through a series of well-planned questions, and in doing so, lead the individual to go up or down on a scale of emotions he had designed to match those same frequencies.

The ridicule of Scientology and the experiments conducted by Hubbard, don't invalidate the effectiveness, which was proven by Dr. Delgado and his team. For if the experiments of Hubbard allowed to control the mind in order to clear a person from his emotional barriers and mental problems, then the CIA and its team of psychiatrists and researchers, among which Dr. Delgado was included, would seek to do the opposite and use the same studies to control the mind of people.

According to Dr. Pugh, "Dr. Delgado proved through his vast research that individuals are defenseless against direct electrical manipulation of the brain because it deprives the person of the most intimate mechanisms of biological reactivity. By using electrical stimuli, the subject is unable to stop the biological response in his body. A person cannot override what the brain fires for the body to respond to. The individual is therefore rendered completely helpless.

This discovery led to the 1960's investigation into the strategy of directing microwave beams at targeted human beings from a distance. These studies found that microwave (ELF) beams created enormous anxiety and hyperactivity in those targeted, so much so, that it led to their complete physical exhaustion."

The fact that Dr. Delgado worked for Yale University — the headquarters of the Skull and Bones Society, is not a coincidence either. George H. W. Bush, who was Director of the CIA in 1976, and President of the United States in 1989, had been a student at Yale University during this period and was initiated

THE ANTICHRIST: THE GRAND PLAN OF TOTAL GLOBAL ENSLAVEMENT

into the Skulls and Bones Society during this time as well. The Yale Daily News (2004) says that, "the CIA has historically proven to be a popular career choice for many Yale graduates, most notably former President George H.W. Bush and legendary operatives William Bundy and James Jesus Angleton."

Undergraduate Career Services Director Philip Jones said (in The Yale Daily News, 2004) that, "It's always been on the radar for Yale students that there is a career in the CIA,... CIA recruiters are frequently on campus, conducting interviews... Information sessions and panels with CIA recruiters are widely attended, generating audiences that range between 70 and 80 students... Of the many Yalies who express interest in working for the CIA each year, the agency typically hires several. And while it is true that other elite institutions, such as Harvard and Princeton, have sent numerous graduates into the ranks of the CIA, Yale's impact on the agency is unparalleled... CIA recruiters visit other college campuses, but they seem to have a predilection for Yalies".

Chapter 72: Beyond The Mind Control Technology.

According to Dr. Joye Jeffries Pugh (In Eden, 2006), "The plan to take over the mind of humans has been developed in stages. It has been going on for quite some time, and uniquely, it incorporates much of Tesla's technology.

The intent of Satan's Plan is to take away a person's capability of recognizing the difference between good and evil, thereby hindering their biological ability to exhibit freedom of choice. It is an evil system designed to allow the politically correct and so-called illuminated men to make all decisions for you and your family with their free will, while robbing you of yours.

This has been Satan's ancient agenda; to create a collective consciousness that will ensure evil progresses without defiance by Christians."

In 1976, the United States Senate, had already become aware of such technology. In a report on Surveillance Technology, a Defense Intelligence Agency review of Soviet literature acknowledges microwave hearing and the possibility for word transmission with potential for "disorientating or disrupting" personnel behavior pattern.

A research later conducted by Oskar, K.J., on the 'Effects of low power microwaves on the local cerebral blood flow of conscious rats' (1980), showed that, "By proper choice of pulse characteristics, intelligible speech may be created" by microwave hearing for "camouflage, decoy, and deception operations"

Then, in 1988, a US Army Intelligence and Security Command Freedom of Information Act (FOIA) release on the 'Bioeffects of Selected Nonlethal Weapons', said that an "Application of the microwave hearing technology could facilitate a private message transmission. . . . it could be psychologically devastating if one suddenly heard 'voices within one's head.'"

In 1989, Brunkan W.B. registered patent US4877027A, as a "Hearing system".

The description of this patent says that, "Sound is induced in the head of a person by radiating the head with microwaves in the range of 100 megahertz to 10,000 megahertz that are modulated with a particular waveform. The waveform consists of frequency modulated bursts... The bursts are frequency modulated by the audio input to create the sensation of hearing in the person whose head is irradiated... This invention relates to a hearing system for human beings in which high frequency electromagnetic energy is projected through the air to the head of a human being and the electromagnetic energy is modulated to create signals that can be discerned by the human being regardless of the hearing ability of the person."

Thanks to this device and 5G, "hearing "voices" can now become a common thing, and no longer attributed merely to either schizophrenia or demonic possession.

In fact, according to the researchers Robert O. Becker and Gary Selden, authors of 'The Body Electric' (1985), this technology can be used to "Drive a target crazy with voices or deliver undetectable instructions to a programmed assassin".

Since then, many reports have shown that the CIA is developing what is called a Microwave Auditory Effect — manufactured microwave voice transmission devices — also known as "voice synthesis" or "synthetic telepathy."

The effective implementation of such technology justifies the need for what Bill Gates termed ID2020, and which according to him are: "Digital certificates saying who is a recovered person and who is a vaccinated person."

Even though Gates is trying to use ID2020 as an excuse to create a system of mandatory injection of psychotropic drugs on the world population through vaccines, he knows that such digital implants can facilitate as well the complete obedience to the totalitarian global control being orchestrated with the use of the 5G towers.

In doing this, he and his team, achieve several goals, among which is:

1. A mass sterilization through vaccines;

THE ANTICHRIST: THE GRAND PLAN OF TOTAL GLOBAL ENSLAVEMENT

2. A massive reduction of the world population of up to 3 billion people or more, through both the sterilization process and the cancer induced toxins inside these vaccines;

3. The enslavement of the rest of the population — survivors of the holocaust.

According to Gates, in an interview to the Financial Times (in April 2020), "People act as if they have a choice, but they don't have a choice". Which means that he believes that this is a worldwide agenda that will come to completion sooner or later.

The use of mandatory vaccination will certainly also accelerate the use of nanotechnology through the vaccines.

In Eden (2006), Dr. Joye Jeffries Pugh explains that, "Vaccines are being developed that will incorporate the use of nanotechnology… with bio-weapons being manufactured by terrorists that target certain races, the nanotech vaccine can be a successful, as well as sinister, antidote. In this case, the vaccine seeks out a genetic marker to rid those that carry certain genes that are being targeted by terrorists, thereby killing the person who has those genes.

These bio-weapons are set up to target certain individuals and therefore will not set up a contagious disease process to spread uncontrollably to others. This form on nano-death could be targeted at any genetic market, such as those with certain diseases, particular races, blood types, etc. No one would be safe if they carried the targeted market that was chosen to be eradicated".

In 2020, Microsoft, in a partnership with VeriChip, also registered patent WO2020060606 — or more simply, Mark 666 — which allows the use of a "Cryptocurrency System Using Body Activity Data". This microchip will then permit to also easily starve dissents to death by simply invalidating the use of their credits, as credits is just another word of digital currency — already popularized and tested through different video games and applications.

Chapter 73: The Use of Games by Intelligence Agencies.

During the early stages on Facebook, The Pentagon was already collecting information from around the globe. Documents declassified by Edward Snowden, and published by the New York Times, show that, "The Pentagon's Special Operations Command in 2006 worked with several foreign companies to build games that could be downloaded to mobile phones… the games, which were not identified as creations of the Pentagon, were then used as vehicles for Intelligence Agencies to collect information about the users."

In 2007, NSA officials met with the chief technology officer of Linden Lab — makers of Second Life — Cory Ondrejka, who said: "Virtual worlds gave the government the opportunity to understand the motivation, context and consequent behaviors of non-Americans through observation, without leaving U.S. soil."

According to documents provided by Snowden, by the end of 2008, the British spy agency, known as GCHQ, had set up its "First operational deployment into Second Life and had helped the police in London in cracking down on a crime ring that had moved into virtual worlds to sell stolen credit card information. They were aided by an informer using a digital avatar who helpfully volunteered information on the target group's latest activities."

In 2013, an article created in partnership between The New York Times, the Guardian and ProPublica — based on the documents disclosed by former NSA contractor Edward J. Snowden —, also reported that, "American and British spies have infiltrated the fantasy worlds of World of Warcraft and Second Life, conducting surveillance and scooping up data in the online games played by millions of people across the globe."

The article then continues by saying that, "Documents show, intelligence operatives have entered terrain populated by digital avatars… The spies have created make-believe characters to snoop and to try to recruit informers, while also collecting data and contents of communications between players."

The article says that CIA, FBI and Pentagon spies were so abundant that a "deconfliction group" was needed to avoid collisions between them.

Even though many companies refused to either confirm or deny such activities, namely, Microsoft, Blizzard Entertainment — the maker of World of Warcraft — was referred by CNBC (2013) as publicly stating that neither the NSA nor their British counterparts had gotten permission to gather intelligence in its game. They claimed to be "unaware of any surveillance taking place,.. and if it was, it would have been done without permission".

The Intelligence Agencies also found other benefits in infiltrating these online worlds, namely, the identification of engineers, embassy drivers, scientists and other foreign intelligence operatives, who are players and potential targets for recruitment as agents.

The documents provided by Snowden say that, at on point, British intelligence officers vacuumed up three days' worth of Second Life chat, instant message and financial transaction data, totaling 176,677 lines of data, which included the content of the communications.

According to Snowden, eager to cash in on the government's growing interest in virtual worlds, several large private contractors have spent years pitching their services to US Intelligence Agencies.

In a document from 2007, declassified by Snowden, one company promoted its ability to support "intelligence collection in the game space," and said that online games could be used by militant groups to recruit followers and could provide "terrorist organizations with a powerful platform to reach core target audiences."

The CIA and Mossad would certainly see a great advantage in this. For it provided the ground-base to recruit both American soldiers and terrorist militants from around the world, allowing to build a network of fanatics that could be motivated to overthrow governments in the middle-east.

THE ANTICHRIST: THE GRAND PLAN OF TOTAL GLOBAL ENSLAVEMENT

In a research article about "Terrorism and Political Violence" (2018), Ahmed Al-Rawi says that, "According to US intelligence experts, about 1000 foreign fighters join ISIS every month… and a number of games directly deal with terror-related issues, especially in connection with the War on Terror… allowing players to become terrorists, which could have some psychological and educational benefits". But, these so-called "educational benefits" would be sought by different groups to fulfill their own agendas.

Ahmed Al-Rawi, says that, "In 2006, the Al-Qaeda group made changes to the first person shooter (FPS) game 'Quest for Saddam' (2003) and introduced another game called Quest for Bush. The goal of the original game was to kill Iraqi soldiers and capture Saddam Hussein, whereas Al-Qaeda completely reversed the players' roles…

On the other hand, video games by the Lebanese Hezbollah and Syrian Afkar Media company were used as alternative media outlets to offer playing roles that were contrary to the mainstream Western representation of Arab Muslims.

In this way, "video games provide violent non-state actors and organizations sympathetic to them with a means of presenting their grievances and displaying their fighting prowess in ways that advance the organizations' strategic goals."

The influence of the Secret Intelligence Agencies such as the CIA and Mossad, were most likely visible in a video game that promoted ISIS terrorism, and was adapted from the well-known Grand Theft Auto (GTA). For, according to Ahmed Al-Rawi, "It is not clear who exactly developed it since there are many links to the video game, especially those leading to torrent websites. However, the current links either do not work or lead to malicious websites. Certainly, the video game's trailer is not produced by the centralized media centers of ISIS like Al-Hayat, Al-Furqan, and Al-Ethar, especially in that the group stands against entertainment activities like listening to music or playing games that can divert attention from prayer and faith".

It is also alleged that ISIS adapted a first person shooter game called RMA III which is developed for Microsoft.

The same article mentions that, "Violent video games are more appealing for adolescents than for adults, partly due to the wishful identification with some of the games' characters. Some view ISIS as a "cool" organization in its Jihad 3.0 efforts, so producing such games can help in recruiting young people to its organization".

The application of games as mind control tools continues to be explored. According to Nick Yee, a Palo Alto researcher who worked on the effort to coordinate video game developers and Secret Agencies goals, they were "Specifically asked not to speculate on the government's motivations and goals."

Chapter 74: How Facebook Became A Global Threat.

Through IQT, Secret Intelligence Services have been investing in companies that serve the purpose of global surveillance and control, namely, for projects like Google Earth.

The Business Insider (2016), says that "In-Q-Tel (named after "Q" in the James Bond films) invests in companies that can deliver useful technology to the intelligence community... typically does not disclose the amount it invests, though a Washington Post story from 2005 says the funding is often relatively small $500,000 to $2 million investments.

The same article also named 14 cutting edge firms funded by the CIA through In-Q-Tel, among which is..

- Orbital Insight — "Analyzes the millions of satellite images being beamed back to Earth to answer all kinds of 'interesting questions'";

- Fuel3d — "Captures highly-detailed three dimensional imagery of rooms, objects, or people";

- MindMeld — "It is a voice recognition technology like Siri — 'for everything'";

- SnapDNA — "It is a handheld device that can analyze DNA in minutes";

- Sonitus — "A wireless, two-way communications capability hidden inside the mouth";

- BBN Technologies — "Allows troops overseas to quickly translate foreign languages".

In 2018, Jody Chudley (Financial Analyst at The Daily Edge), revealed Facebook's CIA Connections through IQT.

According to Chudley, "As far back as 2005, The Washington Post reported that virtually any U.S. entrepreneur, inventor or research scientist working on ways to analyze data had probably received a phone call from In-Q-Tel or at least been Googled by its staff of technology watchers. One company that happened to be very hungry for startup capital in 2005 was Facebook.

Facebook was launched in February 2004 from the Harvard dorm room of Mark Zuckerberg and friends. The company received its first capital injection of $500,000 from Peter Thiel that summer. The next two capital injections were $12.7 million from Thiel and Accel Partners in May 2005 and then $27.5 million from an Accel-led round of financing that included Thiel, Accel and Greylock Partners in April 2006".

Each one of the investors on Facebook had connections to In-Q-Tel. According to the same article:

- "Peter Thiel — Took In-Q-Tel funding for his startup firm Palantir somewhere around 2004.

- Accel Partners — In 2004, Accel partner James Breyer sat on the board of directors of military defense contractor BBN with In-Q-Tel's CEO Gilman Louie.

- Greylock Partners — Howard Cox, the head of Greylock, served directly on In-Q-Tel's board of directors."

Back in 2004, a very arrogant but still very young Mark Zuckerberg, gave an interview to CNBC about Facebook, in which he revealed the purpose of his platform, when saying the following:

"We were trying to fill a gap... creating applications that should keep people coming to the site and maybe make something cool... You make a profile about yourself by answering some questions and giving up some information... Most importantly, who your friends are... and then you can browse around and check people's 'identities'... and check information about people."

THE ANTICHRIST: THE GRAND PLAN OF TOTAL GLOBAL ENSLAVEMENT

What he was actually saying between words, is that he already knew he would become a millionaire within just two years, by collecting private data from around the globe and then sell it to the CIA through In-Q-Tel for about $40 Million.

His real purpose, at that point, was actually to create a platform that could guarantee a continuous harvesting of data, that he would then sell to private corporations, business advertisers and the CIA, in order to multiply his fortune for the years to come.

In 2007, Bill Gates, through Microsoft, bought a share of Facebook for $240 Million. And in 2016, Newspunch said that both George Soros and Bill Gates where funding Facebook's Fact Checkers, e.g., information censorship and bias totalitarian control.

The use and abuse of private information also seems to be the question Mark Zuckerberg — CEO of Facebook — avoids the most.

In a EU testimony, Zuckerberg was repeatedly asked about "Shadow Profiles" — the obtaining of private information that wasn't voluntarily given to Facebook:

"How do you stop that data from being transferred?"

Mark Zuckerberg refused to answer the question.

According to Laura Hautala, (in CNET, 2018), "Facebook amasses information on you that you didn't hand over yourself. That can happen whether or not you're a Facebook user."

According to the same article, this was later confirmed by Zuckerberg who said:

"In general, we collect data of people who have not signed up for Facebook for security purposes."

The article continues, saying that, "If you gave the social network access to the contacts in your phone, it could have taken your mom's second email address and added it to the information your mom already gave to Facebook herself.

During the time of the data breach, your mom might then have downloaded her information from Facebook, only to find that second email address listed by her name."

In an attempt at explaining how the contact data eventually get leaked, Zuckerberg said:

"When people upload their contact lists or address books to Facebook, we try to match that data with the contact information of other people on Facebook in order to generate friend recommendations."

According to Laura Gowans, chief operating officer of privacy-oriented tech company SpiderOak, "The problem is if my friend uses that app and has my contact info, she's consented and I haven't, but Facebook still has my information,... It's really, really hard to control what information of your own is getting out there,... you would have to maintain a fake phone number, or never give anybody your phone number or address for any reason".

The main problem that Facebook raises is that it's collecting data from around the world, with or without people's consent, and handing it directly to the Intelligence Agencies. And in doing so, Facebook has become an international threat.

It is actually for this reason that China doesn't allow its internet users to access this platform.

Nonetheless, China has been using this type of technology to move forward in its plans to control its people and eliminate any dissents.

Many of the political prisoners of China were caught through their own platforms, such as QQ, WeChat and Weibo.

Everything else is blocked by the Communists: Google, Facebook, Instagram, Pinterest, Twitter, WhatsApp, and so on.

Chapter 75: How the AI Monitors Thoughts and Emotions.

In 2018, Tara Francis Chan revealed (In The Business Insider), that China is monitoring employees' brain waves and emotions, and that the technology boosted one company's profits by $315 million. She said that, "The technology works by placing wireless sensors in employees' caps or hats which, combined with artificial intelligence algorithms, spot incidents of workplace rage, anxiety, or sadness. Employers use this 'emotional surveillance technology' by then tweaking workflows, including employee placement and breaks, to increase productivity and profits".

According to the South China Morning Post, more than a dozen businesses and China's military have used a different programme developed by the government-funded brain surveillance project NeuroCap, based out of Ningbo University.

According to, Jin Jia, Professor of Brain Science at Ningbo University (In South China Morning Post), "People thought we could read their mind. This caused some discomfort and resistance in the beginning, but after a while they got used to the device... They wore it all day at work. When the system issues a warning, the manager asks the worker to take a day off or move to a less critical post... Employees' brainwaves can be enough for managers to send them home, as their productivity is measured and monitored in "brainwaves" rather than hours."

The same device was also used in primary schools. In 2019, the South China Morning Post, reported that "Brain scanning headbands to measure students attention spans" where being used to monitor student's activity in the classroom.

This can be what the bible meant by having the mark of the beast in the forehead (Revelation 13:16), as the reference to the right hand is most likely related to the same technology — through a microchip implant.

According to Business Insider, "Widespread use of emotion monitoring may mark a new stage in China's surveillance state, which has largely been focused on facial recognition and increasing internet censorship. It's unknown if all employees subjected to the technology are aware they are being monitored, but even if they were, China's privacy laws would be unlikely to help. The notoriously lax privacy laws, and the country's large sample population, have helped China leap ahead with its artificial intelligence research... China applied for five times as many AI patents as the US in 2017."

Chapter 76: The Mark 666 and Nanotechnology.

According to the reference in Revelation 13 (In the Bible), "No man might buy or sell, save he that had the mark, or the name of the beast, or the number of his name... his number is Six hundred threescore and six", which means that we are likely going to merge the Rothschild Banking System and the Gates Foundation, through ID2020 and Microsoft patent 666.

Dr. Joye Jeffries Pugh confirmed this plan in her the book "Eden" (2006), when she says that, "The desire to control the world has been the ongoing goal of the Elite within Secret Societies. One of their own, Dr. José Delgado, Professor at Yale University, where the famous Skull and Bones Order is located, said, "We need a program of psychosurgery for political control of your society. The purpose is physical control of the mind. Everyone who deviates from the given norm can be surgically mutilated.

The individual may think that the most important reality is his own existence, but this is only his personal point of view... Man does not have the right to develop his own mind... We must electronically control the brain. Someday armies and generals will be controlled by electronic stimulation of the brain".

This technology would then allow creating armies of super soldiers, without any conscience or empathy whatsoever, like cyborgs, as portrayed in the movie 'Universal Soldier'. But would we truly need such soldiers?

According to Dr. Pugh, the use of mandatory vaccines, would incorporate nanotech, which would then allow eliminating dissents, and even specific people, with a very high precision — using DNA codes —, but also change the brain of anyone with specific signals, and based on the experiments of Dr. José Delgado.

Dr. Pugh says that, "With the science of Nanotechnology in the wrong hands, dissenters will be faced with two choices after they have been implanted. That is, to either be surgically slaughtered internally by nanorobots for failing to follow the Antichrist, or simply just following the Antichrist out of fear of being internally slaughtered. Either way, one must follow the New World Order or their death will be immediately programmed and the robots will take action toward that end.

Those around the person will think the individual died due to natural causes and will never suspect what is really going on.

As nanorobots are perfected, they will have the capacity to attack the brain and damage areas where human emotions exist. They will produce an instant solution to the control of any rebel not willing to go along with the New World Order.

The positive aspects of what nanorobotics can offer humanity will continually be promoted without referencing the potential horrors of the technology... Nanorobots will have the ability to surgically cut and take biopsies internally, while immediately evaluating the tissue. These procedures will be done with the person fully awake, with no need for anesthetics."

Chapter 77: The Last Days on Earth.

The book of Revelation says that the first beast comes "out of the sea" and is given authority and power by the dragon. It then says (In Revelation 13:1-10) that, "They worshipped the dragon which gave power unto the beast".

If we consider this dragon to be a country, we know that the only country represented by a dragon with enough power to submit others to its will is China.

As for the mystery behind the appearance of the beast, it is mentioned in Revelation 17: "I will tell thee the mystery of the woman, and of the beast that carrieth her, which hath the seven heads and ten horns."

This is certainly a metaphor to the European Union, which is represented by a woman riding a bull. The EU parliament in Brussels even has this statue as their mascot.

According to the Book of Revelation, the second beast comes "out of the Earth" and directs all peoples of the Earth to worship the first beast. Still about this second beast, Revelation says that, "He exerciseth all the power of the first beast before him, and causeth the earth and them which dwell therein to worship the first beast, whose deadly wound was healed. And he doeth great wonders, so that he maketh fire come down from heaven on the earth in the sight of men. And deceiveth them that dwell on the earth by the means of those miracles which he had power to do in the sight of the beast; saying to them that dwell on the earth, that they should make an image to the beast, which had the wound by a sword, and did live... he had power to give life unto the image of the beast, that the image of the beast should both speak, and cause that as many as would not worship the image of the beast should be killed."

There is only one nation capable of making the world worship the first beast — Europe —, and that is the United Sates. As for the wound that is healed, it is probably a reference to an atomic bomb hitting Europe.

The Book of Revelation says that the two beasts are aligned with the dragon in opposition to God. They persecute the "saints" and those who do "not worship the image of the beast [of the sea] and influence the kings of the earth to gather for the battle of Armageddon." And these two beasts aligned with the dragon in opposition to God, are most likely references to a union between Europe, the United States and China. The saints they persecute are the empaths that this book has clearly identified.

These empaths are very few, and they will most certainly refuse the policies and laws of the two beasts and the dragon.

Even though we could identify a false prophet as the Antichrist, the bible seems to guide us towards symbols of powers. In this sense, the Antichrist is most likely the AI — Artificial Intelligence —, through which Satan can manifest himself.

Those in power, being atheists, will think that they are receiving orders from a computer, when in fact they will be receiving their orders from Satan himself. The majority of the psychopaths in power are possessed by demons anyway, so they will follow this AI blindly. And the AI will control all of the Earth, through frequencies, signals and nanotechnology. These frequencies and nanorobots, will control people's mind and facilitate demonic possession at a much larger scale, making it automatic. But could Satan communicate through frequencies and the AI?

We should notice that, one of reasons that led the CIA to infiltrate Scientology, is because the founder was trying to study the correlation between demonic possession and what he termed "tone levels" — a technical word for the frequencies that emanate from our bodies, and that in other faiths are known as an aura.

The book of Revelation also continues on describing that, "The two beasts are defeated by Christ and are then thrown into the lake of fire" (In Revelation 19:18). This lake of fire is again another metaphor for the destruction that

THE ANTICHRIST: THE GRAND PLAN OF TOTAL GLOBAL ENSLAVEMENT

the United States and Europe will face, not through Christ, but the Christian Consciousness, manifesting itself on Earth as a conglomerate of spaceships from many other planets and galaxies.

According to Paul Hellyer — former Chadian Minister of National Defence — "All worlds in the galaxy are interconnected. What happens in one planet affects the others". As such, it is likely that the habitants of the other worlds wouldn't just allow for a complete AI takeover on the Earth to occur. The aliens — or angels —, would come to the aid of those in need.

The Bible confirms this, in Matthew 24, when it says: "He shall send his angels with a great sound of a trumpet, and they shall gather together his elect from the four winds, from one end of heaven to the other... Heaven and earth shall pass away, but my words shall not pass away. But of that day and hour knoweth no man, no, not the angels of heaven, but my Father only. But as the days of Noah were, so shall also the coming of the Son of man be... Then shall two be in the field; the one shall be taken, and the other left. Two women shall be grinding at the mill; the one shall be taken, and the other left."

The angels are aliens that come to the aid of the "elect" or the empaths of Earth. It says that, "As the days of Noah were, so shall also the coming of the Son of man be" because, as in the days of Noah, the narcissists, the psychopaths and the wicked, shall all be eliminated, to empty the Earth for a new beginning on the right path — of love, compassion and empathy with all living creatures, in this planet and beyond, as a big and galactic family.

"One shall be taken, and the other left", is a reference to the ones who shall be rescued — through mass alien abdications — amidst the turmoil and wars that will be promoted by the two beasts and the dragon — most likely an attempt of the AI (led by Satan), at directing the entire world into a world war to exterminate mankind.

Chapter 78: The Secret Space Program.

The Secret Intelligence has always been interested in religions that promote the belief in extraterrestrials, because they come closer to what is termed 'Christ Consciousness'. And they seek to replace it, with the AI — which will depend on a mass atheism to be followed, or otherwise people wouldn't blindly trust a machine to tell them what to do — and also by using their own Earthly built UFOs — controlled by humans presenting themselves later as aliens.

The persistence of the Shadow Government in trying to keep the Earthly UFOs a secret, is also a strong indicator that they may be preparing to use them in a war against a foreign invasion from space — to stop the biblical prophecy from fulfilling itself.

Dr. Carol Rosin, who worked closely with Wernher Von Braun — former nazi scientist brought to the US through project paperclip to work with NASA — said that, according to him, there would an alien invasion hoax. The goal of this hoaxed space alien invasion was simple: "Control through fear, to drive governments of all nations to submit and unite under one central authority, a One World Government."

The evidence of this is presented in the constant conditioning that is perpetrated by the many movies showing aliens as threatening and predatory. Such films as "Independence Day," "Alien", "War of the Worlds" and others produced by Hollywood studios have had their effect on the subconscious mind of the general public.

As Dr. Greer states in his interviews, "This mental conditioning to fear ET has been subtly reinforced for decades, in preparation for future deceptions".

Wernher von Braun's assistant, Dr. Carol Rosin, and Dr. Steven Greer of The Disclosure Project, have been trying to warn the world at large of this coming deception based on secret energy technology, new visual projection technology and the continued demonization of space aliens by the media and the military industrial complex.

According to Dr. Greer, "Space based weapons are already in place – part of a secret parallel space program that has been operating since the 1960s. ARVs are built and ready to go. Space holographic deception technologies are in place, tested and ready to fire. And the Big Media is a pawn..."

Paul Hellyer said that, "We know that the technology exists, but unfortunately, the same people who were making us poor, are controlling what is happening in the world and in the United States. They own the oil companies and they don't want competition in that field, and they have big stakes in the pharmaceutical companies and the healing industry, and they don't want us to have the kind of healing that is considered a miracle because it is way ahead of us. The aliens are ahead of us in medicine, agriculture, as well as technology. And we should be reaping the benefits of this because they came to help us. They said it: "We are here to help you, if you let us." And so, it is power and greed, not national security the problem... and we have to have disclosure because the stakes are too high to fail."

Despite the secrecy, an exchange of information and technology between some species of aliens — that are aligned with the goals of the Shadow Government — and humans, has been occurring for a very long time. In one case, that is reported, humans actually visited an alien planet.

Paul Hellyer said that, "It has been revealed by the military that an exchange was real as depicted in a movie of Spielberg, in a program referred to as 'Operation Crystal Night', also known as Serpo Project — claiming that 12 astronauts left Earth in july 1965 and where taken to the planet Serpo, in the binary star system Zeta Reticuli, in an alien ship as part of an exchange project..."

Chapter 79: The Angels of Christ.

Unfortunately, the vast majority of the Christians and Muslims of today, are so immersed in metaphors, that can't comprehend how they apply to real life. They are so obsessed with the idea of angels with wings, that they can't believe in aliens. And even though they worship an alien being — a God, they claim not to believe in aliens.

This mass ignorance called faith is so absurd that it keeps them blind to the real meaning and purpose of their faith, for it has been clearly exposed by their books. In the Gospel of Judas (280 AD), for example, a conversation occurs, in which Jesus says the following to Judas:

— "It is impossible to sow seed in rock and harvest its fruit. Come, so that I may teach you about secrets that no other person has seen, for there exists a great and boundless realm, whose extent no generation of angels has seen, in which there is a great invisible Spirit, which no eye of an angel has ever seen, no thought of the heart has ever comprehended, and that was never called by any name."

Jesus was speaking to Judas about the vastness of the Universe and its many manifestations of life. And he wanted to show this to Judas, by boarding a UFO with him as the scripture shows:

"Upon saying this, a luminous cloud appeared there, and Jesus continued,

— Let an angel come into being as my attendant.

Then a great angel, an enlightened of the Divine Self-generated, emerged from the cloud. And following him, four other angels came into being from another cloud, and they became attendants for the Angelic Self-generated. And he said:

— Look, you have been told everything. Lift up your eyes and look at the cloud and the light within it and the stars surrounding it. The star that leads the way is your star.

Jesus lifted up his eyes and saw the luminous cloud, and they entered it."

These references to alien spaceships and to communications between angels — or aliens — and the apostles or Jesus, are abundant in many gospels, reason why they were removed from the Bible.

The Bible that the Christians follow today, is the compilation of manuscripts that the Vatican selected as a reference to their teachings. It is not the full compilation of gospels available at the time. Most were prohibited! And yet, the Christians of today, no matter which religions they agree to follow, are all blindly following the same book.

Jesus explained this ignorance of the christians and other religious groups very well, when he says: "It is impossible to sow seed in rock and harvest its fruit." And then, the gospel continues: "Upon saying this, a luminous cloud appeared there". Which is a clear indication to a UFO.

Jesus continued, saying: "Let an angel come into being as my attendant!" Which, again, has to be logically addressed as an extraterrestrial, and not some mystical creature with wings.

The Gospel then says: "A great angel, an enlightened of the Divine Self-generated, emerged from the cloud." Yes, an alien being came out of the spaceship. "And following him, four other angels came into being from another cloud"; meaning, other aliens came also from their own spaceship to join with Jesus and Judas.

The phrase, "Lift up your eyes and look at the cloud and the light within it and the stars surrounding it", is a clear reference to the lights emerging from the grayish metallic UFO.

"Jesus lifted up his eyes and saw the luminous cloud, and they entered it"; meaning that both, Jesus and Judas, boarded the UFOs.

The reason as to why this information keeps being hidden from the public may be precisely related to the implications it can have at many levels, namely, for governments and the many religions from around the world. Because, the inability in people to believe in a bigger and intergalactic family, as well as their lack of capacity to interpret their own religious texts, as they were meant to be interpreted, rather than accepting the metaphors as they are, would certainly lead to a great opposition and maybe wars, not only against the alien beings but also against governments supporting them.

In our times, many Christians actually believe that the UFOs are demonic demonstrations and the aliens, demons is disguise; and to this, I must say, when stupidity reaches such levels of absurdity, it is impossible to, as Jesus said, "obtain any fruit from rock", e.g., any logical conclusion from any seed — conversation or argument.

You can't talk to rocks and expect an answer, in the same way that you can't explain logic to the very ignorant, that insist on believing in metaphors and fairytales, and expect them to understand.

Chapter 80: The Judgement Day.

We can try to understand our situation, through what the aliens themselves told us. According to Paul Hellyer, they said the following to one of our representatives on Earth:

"Yes, it is true that we have been in contact with your government and other people in power. It is also true that we have made agreements that are kept secret from your people. It is also true that, in the past, some of your people have lost their lives, or have been badly hurt to protect the secret. Our hands have no part in this. We contacted your leaders because your planet is in grave trouble. Your leaders said the vast majority of your population wasn't ready for anything like us yet. And so, we made time agreements with your leaders, as to when your people would be made aware of our presence. But this part of the agreement has not at all been kept.

There was also the agreement that measures would be taken to correct the environment condition of your planet with our advice and technology. We say advice, because we respect the fact that this is your planet, not ours. They also broke this agreement.

Your air and your water are contaminated! Your forest, jungles, trees and planet life are dying. There are several breaks in your food chain. You have an overwhelming amount of nuclear and biological weapons, which include nuclear and biological contamination. Your planet is overpopulated. It is coming to the point of being too late, unless your people act.

There are better ways of deriving energy and food needs without causing your planet any damage. Those in power are aware of this and have the capability to put these methods into worldwide use. Those in power view it as a military and security threat. Government and leaders have been suppressing the truth and they can't be hold liable for the past deeds. This is the only way these leaders can come forward with the truth. It is necessary that you do this in order to work together and survive."

As the agreements have been broken, the extraterrestrials have been working through individuals to try and get the message out, in the hope that we will take their warning seriously, and that somehow, we will be able to transmit the urgency to our leaders and to get them to act before it is too late.

Meanwhile, the Elite continues with their plans, as the goal of most of the members behind this conspiracy is to merge their identity with the AI and live forever, in a kind of Borg Society, in which they are the immortal leaders of slaves.

This is possible, if we consider that this Antichrist is actually an artificial program, that will incorporate the identity of these leaders, and then download them to clone bodies, allowing them to live forever, through bodies that keep being replaced, as we have seen in many fiction movies, and that are now becoming a reality. The rest of society will not have the right to eternal life, unless they obey this AI-God. And for that to happen, they must wear the mark of the beast — the microchip.

The AI, or "Satan's Technology", would then merge humanity, and allow the demonic world to manifest itself fully, through frequencies and implantable microchips. And such world will truly be the world of Satan.

Those who are now in power, most of which are possessed by demons themselves, are being deceived as much as they deceive others, into accepting such reality. Their ambition for immortality, even though motivated by their atheist beliefs and knowledge about technology, will actually merge them with the Antichrist — the Technological God or AI Borg Machine.

This plan is being put in practice through many philanthropic agendas, just as the Bible warns. For it says, in Romans 16:18, "With good words and fair speeches they'll deceive the hearts of the ignorant".

Indeed, the ignorant, as this book has showed you, will be destroyed. Even Jesus warned us of the same, when saying: "My people are destroyed because they lack knowledge" (Hosea 4:6).

THE ANTICHRIST: THE GRAND PLAN OF TOTAL GLOBAL ENSLAVEMENT

This knowledge has been fully presented to you in this book and through the Holy Spirit, if you so choose to believe.

I am also convinced that, if Jesus was alive today, and was a North American, he would certainly speak differently and more directly, and say to you: "You die cause y'all so damn stupid."

Those who can see, already know that we are heading towards the creation of a Borg Society on Earth, based on a pyramid structure with the Power Elite at the top, as cybernetic gods with eternal life merged with the AI, and controlling the rest of the planet — the cyborg slaves.

The chosen ones — spiritual, awaken, enlightened, empathic — shall be removed from this Technocratic Earth, before the whole insanity is destroyed by the Galactic Confederation, whose teachings were promoted on Earth by Christ, in an attempt to guide us towards more compassion and love.

The Confederation will then — as representatives of the Cosmic Consciousness or Christian Consciousness — annihilate the Anti-christian Borg in a massive fire. And the chosen ones will be divided in two groups, between the ones who choose to restart and repopulate the Earth with the help of the Confederation, and those who wish to live abroad, on other planets and galaxies (as was confirmed by members of the Jehovah Witnesses, and many other Christian groups, and according to the prophecy explained to them by "their real leaders".

Chapter 81: God and the Gods.

There's something that people have to understand in regards to the Antichrist and the symbolism of the goat head, and that's that it represents the attachments to the Earth.

Satan does not want humans to evolve as spiritual beings and ascend. As such, anything that implies attachment is part of the anti-christian plan. And yes, it includes the lies told by many biblical religions, in order to keep the followers from embracing a wider perspective of life — encompassing all of the universal life, and not just the one present on Earth.

The idea that God only created humans and life on Earth is a lie that intends to keep the Christians attached to this belief and closed to the true Christianity as was taught by Jesus Christ.

In many ancient texts, the original reference, from which they were translated, using words such as angels or Gods, says something else. "Sons of the Gods (From the Hebrew: בני האלהים, romanized: bənê ĕlōhîm, literally means "sons of the gods") is a phrase used in the Hebrew Bible and in Christian Apocrypha. The phrase is also used in Kabbalah where bene elohim are part of different Jewish angelic hierarchies" (In Wikipedia).

Few people also know that, when Jesus said, "I am the son of Elohim (the gods), he went further, to say (In Psalms 82:6), "You are gods, and all of you are children of the Most High — The Elohim (the gods or "mighty ones", or quite simply, "powerful human beings")."

Although many may argue about the real meaning of the words, the original New Testament manuscripts translate Christ's quotation in John 10 using the Greek word theoi—"gods." And so, it is obvious that Jesus did meant "gods" and not "God".

The reference to the gods, is mentioned as well in Genesis, when after creating plants and animals to reproduce each "according to its kind," God said: "Let Us make man in Our image, according to Our likeness" — showing that man was created according to the "gods" as a collective, and not one as a singularity.

In Acts 17:28, it says that Paul told the men of Athens, "We are also His offspring' "

We must understand, nonetheless, that humans are not yet like those who created them. Humanity is still evolving. And the antithesis of this christian-like attitude is in fact to refuse this natural evolution by merging with machines. For the evolution occurs first at a spiritual level, before it manifests at a physical level.

Therefore, to say that humans were created at the image of the gods, is to say that humans can develop towards becoming as the rest of the galactic family — more spiritual, more loving, more compassionate, more wise, and so on.

This does not invalidate the existence of a God. On the contrary, it reinforces it, by merging the Earthly family into the collective consciousness represented by all the other galactic families.

When in Romans 8:16, it says that, "The Spirit itself beareth witness with our spirit, that we are the children of God", and then, in Peter 1:4, "Through this miraculous union, we become "partakers of the divine nature", both quotes address our spiritual union with the "families from the whole universe".

This fact was shown in Ante-Nicene Fathers (AD 200) — a collection of books containing English translations of the majority of Early Christian writings.

It regards to Peter 1:4, it was translated in the following way:

"We will be even gods, if we deserve to be among those of whom He declared, 'I have said, "You are gods,"' and 'God stands in the congregation of the gods.' But this comes of His own grace, not from any property in us. For it is He alone who can make gods"

THE ANTICHRIST: THE GRAND PLAN OF TOTAL GLOBAL ENSLAVEMENT

Christianity is not a polytheistic religion. But this christian God is a living consciousness. Therefore, the term gods is really meant to distinguish multiple God Beings representing the one God, as a one God family.

In Galatians 3:26, it says: "You are all sons of God through faith in Christ Jesus." And what this means is that, through faith in the christian message, we become united with the rest of the sons of God.

This said, in which way could we then refuse God?

By refusing our faith — through atheism and a lack of consciousness — and by refusing the Christian message — love and unity with the rest of the spiritual family.

This denial can indeed occur, as mentioned before, with the wrong faith and the wrong beliefs. Reason why this book had to be written. It is both in accordance to scripture and the events we are witnessing.

One path leads us to imprisonment, without empathy or love; the other path leads us much higher, towards the embracing of everyone on Earth and the rest of the community of souls in space.

Per aspera ad astra — through hardships to the stars!

Bibliography

Becker, Robert O. & Selden, Gary. 'The Body Electric: Electromagnetism And The Foundation Of Life'. William Morrow, 1998.

Black, Edwin. 'Eugenics'. Dialog Press, 2012.

Critchlow, Donald T.. 'The Politics of Abortion and Birth Control in Historical Perspective'. Penn State University Press, 1996.

Han, Byung-Chul. 'Pychopolitics'. Verso, 2017.

Harrison, Barbara G.. 'Visions of Glory: A History and a Memory of Jehovah's Witnesses', Simon and Schuster, 1978.

Harvey, David. 'Population, Resources, and the Ideology of Science'. Taylor & Francis, Ltd., 1974.

Huxley, Aldous. 'Psychedelic Prophets'. McGill-Queen's University Press, 2018.

Keith, Jim. 'Secret and Suppressed: Banned Ideas and Hidden History'. Feral House, 2008.

Mackey, Albert G.. 'Encyclopedia of Freemasonry'. CreateSpace, 2014.

Maynard, Andrew. 'Films from the Future'. Mango, 2018.

McLuhan, Marshall. 'Culture Is Our Business'. Wipf and Stock, 2015.

Patnaik, Utsa. 'Republic of Hunger'. Merlin Press, 2008.

Péloquin, Marys. Raël: Voleur d'âmes. Trait D'Union, 2004.

Pugh, Dr. Joye Jeffries. 'Eden: The Knowledge Of Good and Evil 666'. Lulu, 2018.

Regardie, Israel. 'The Complete Golden Dawn System of Magic'. New Falcon Publications, 2014.

Steiner, Rudolf. 'The Fall of the Spirits of Darkness'. Rudolf Steiner Press, 1995.

DAN DESMARQUES

Trento, Joseph John. 'The Secret History of the CIA'. Forum, 2001.

Did you love *The Antichrist: The Grand Plan of Total Global Enslavement*? Then you should read *The Secret Empire: The Hidden Truth Behind the Power Elite and the Knights of the New World Order*[1] by Dan Desmarques!

[2]

The world keeps changing extremely fast, but either in times of abundance or scarcity, under persecution or with the control over mankind, many have prospered. And they did so by looking at the patterns of the world in which we live and with the understanding of such patterns.

At the top of this social hierarchy, warlords, totalitarian regimes, kings and queens, through their secret organizations, planned wars that changed the world in specific directions. And all of them claimed to do this in the name of their country, religion, God and even freedom.

However, their hierarchies led to the creation of secret societies but also secret governments and secret agendas, kept away from the general public and discussed in secrecy and in secret meetings. These secrets led to the

---

1. https://books2read.com/u/3yEADl

2. https://books2read.com/u/3yEADl

accumulation of power in many realms of life. In fact, many of the greatest criminals in human history, remain alive and well to this day, still exercising positions of power and great influence in different countries.

This best selling book will show you the facts behind the real history of the world. For the first time ever, many conspiracies are connected and explained in a way that will challenge even the most willing believers. Because the truth is indeed more incredible than many would assume it to be.

This book has been in the best selling charts of Amazon for more than eight years in a row, although previously published under other titles, and there have been many attempts at removing it from the market, but if you found it, you are now presented with an unique opportunity to see what you were never taught in school or allowed to know.

The information presented here is based on a research that has taken more than twenty years to develop. And, for this reason, it resumes a vast amount of complexity in the best way possible.

The awakening that reading this book will cause you, will certainly lead you to a great moment of understanding in your life.

Also by Dan Desmarques

Spiritual Warfare: What You Need to Know About Overcoming Adversity
Collective Consciousness: How to Transcend Mass Consciousness and Become One With the Universe
The Spiritual Mechanics of Love: Secrets They Don't Want You to Know about Understanding and Processing Emotions
The 10 Laws of Transmutation: The Multidimensional Power of Your Subconscious Mind
The Evil Within: The Spiritual Battle in Your Mind
Deception: When Everything You Know about God is Wrong
How to Change the World: The Path of Global Ascension Through Consciousness
Religious Leadership: The 8 Rules Behind Successful Congregations
The 14 Karmic Laws of Love: How to Develop a Healthy and Conscious Relationship With Your Soulmate
A New Way of Being: How to Rewire Your Brain and Take Control of Your Life
Uma Nova Forma de Existir: Como Organizar Sua Mente e Assumir o Controle da Sua Vida
O Propósito da Sua Alma: A Reencarnação e o Espectro da Consciência na Evolução
Your Soul Purpose: Reincarnation and the Spectrum of Consciousness in Human Evolution
Encontre Seu fluxo: Como Adquirir a Sabedoria e o Conhecimento de Deus
Find Your Flow: How to Get Wisdom and Knowledge from God
66 Days to Change Your Life: 12 Steps to Effortlessly Remove Mental Blocks, Reprogram Your Brain and Become a Money Magnet
66 Dias Para Mudar Sua Vida: 12 Etapas Para Remover Bloqueios Mentais, Reprogramar Seu Cérebro e Atrair Dinheiro

Consciência Coletiva: Como Transcender a Consciência de Massa e Se Tornar Um com o Universo

Batalha Espiritual: O Que Você Precisa Saber Para Superar a Adversidade

Codex Illuminatus: Quotes & Sayings of Dan Desmarques

Codex Illuminatus: Citações e Provérbios de Dan Desmarques

As 14 Leis Cármicas do Amor: Como Desenvolver Um Relacionamento Saudável e Consciente Com Sua Alma Gêmea

The Hidden Language of God: How to Find a Balance Between Freedom and Responsibility

Your Full Potential: How to Overcome Fear and Solve Any Problem

The Secret Science of the Soul: How to Transcend Common Sense and Get What You Really Want From Life

?????????????????????

Technocracy: The New World Order of the Illuminati and The Battle Between Good and Evil

The Secret Empire: The Hidden Truth Behind the Power Elite and the Knights of the New World Order

The Antichrist: The Grand Plan of Total Global Enslavement

About the Publisher

This book was published by 22Lions.com.
Follow us at Facebook.com/22lions

www.ingramcontent.com/pod-product-compliance
Lightning Source LLC
Chambersburg PA
CBHW071956070526
44583CB00015B/1214